Fifty Missionary Heroes Every Boy and Girl Should Know

Fifty Missionary Heroes
Every Boy and Girl Should Know

By
JULIA H. JOHNSTON

*" These Heroes of the former days
Deserved and gained their never-fading bays."*

ILLUSTRATED

NEW YORK
Fleming H. Revell Company
LONDON AND EDINBURGH

New York: 158 Fifth Avenue

Inscribed to

The Boys and Girls of our To-Day,
Who fare along Time's opening way,
Still looking forward, blithe and free,
To find what each may do and see.

To you, exuberant with life,
Exultant, even in the strife,
To you, so rich in buoyant hope,
And fearing not with ills to cope,
We look expectantly, and cry
Concerning daytimes passing by.

While thinking of the future track,
Take ample time for looking back
To see where Hero-souls have trod,
Along the way that leads to God —
The path of faith and helpful deeds,
For souls a-thrill with others' needs.

To you, with pulses beating high,
Hath Opportunity come nigh.
What pathways open, wide and far!
Whate'er you do, Whoe'er you are,
Be quick to find and fill your place,
For your To-morrows come apace.

J. H. I.

Peoria, Illinois.

Foreword

THIS rosary of Names which the Christian world will not let die, is presented for the use of boys and girls who are ready for their first lessons in deathless history. The Hero-roll of the whole wide world has furnished these Names, but not all of those worthy of note have been taken, since we cannot use the sky for a scroll.

Stories of those earliest and longest in service have been told; those of a later day have also been included. The aim has been to give some clue to the personality of each, associating the person with the place, rather than to give any detailed account of the work accomplished. Nothing exhaustive has been attempted in any case, for fear of making it exhausting to the readers. The childhood and youth of the characters have been dwelt upon, and available incidents, showing them to have been actual boys and girls, have been told, as of special interest.

The chapters have been arranged with some reference to the order of time in which the heroes and heroines lived upon earth, but only in a general way. The figures given indicate the beginning and end of the missionary service.

These short and simple stories of heroic lives may

be used in various ways, aside from finding a place
in Sunday-school libraries, and upon the shelves of
boy and girl readers. Junior Study Classes may
use the volume as a text-book on Hero-studies.
Mission Circles and Bands may find it feasible to
assign characters from month to month, to be read
at home by members, and given verbally at the
meetings—not read from the pages—oh, no!
"Told" stories are far better.

Material may be found between these covers for
supplemental Sunday-school Class-work. One or
two characters may be taken up on specified Sabbath days, and the scholars asked to give the
salient points in the five-minute period to spare for
such Mission Studies. For younger scholars, the
better plan may be for the teacher to give verbally
and briefly one little sketch at a time, reviewing the
points of the story the next week. Another plan
is to allow scholars to select "favourite heroes or
heroines " and tell the story in their own words to
the class. Those that have been chosen should be
marked in the book, or a list of them written upon
a fly-leaf, so that the same ones will not be repeated
too often. If familiar stories are told again, they
may be made "guess stories," told without men-
tioning the name which is left to be guessed and
given by the hearers.

Missionary interest must begin in young hearts.
and in the fervent desire to help a little in pre-
empting them for The Cause, these little tales of
great Heroes is sent forth by

THE AUTHOR.

Contents

Contents

Contents

I

EARLY MISSIONARIES IN ENGLAND
Probably in the Third Century

DID you ever think that there could be a time when England needed missionaries? How could that be, when we remember that our forefathers, who came from there in the *Mayflower*, and in ships that followed, were such earnest Christians? It is true that they were, but remember that there were hundreds of years of history before the *Mayflower*, and that England could not *always* have been a Christian country. It took a long while for the good news to be carried from Palestine to Rome, and farther on, beyond Italy.

But Christianity was early introduced into England. Gaul (France) had the Gospel first. As early as 208 A. D. Tertullian wrote, "Parts of Britain are subject to Christ." Messengers from Gaul must have told of Jesus. In 314 and 350 A. D. history shows English Bishops present in Councils, indicating the organization of the Church of Britain. Bede the historian mentions St. Martin's Church, where Queen Bertha worshipped, which must have been before 410 A. D.

About the middle of the sixth century Great Britain was overrun by Teutonic, or German races from in and around the Baltic Sea. One of these races was called Angles, and the part of Britain where they settled was called East Anglia. In course of time these Angles spread over the land and gave the name Angleland, finally becoming England, to the whole country. Isn't it interesting?

Well, in those days of wars and all sorts of terrible things, slavery was common almost everywhere. When men became so poor that they could not pay their debts, and had nothing to live on, they often sold themselves into slavery. Sometimes their creditors sold them for slaves. Many, many times, captives taken in battle were sold, even in other countries. One day a new lot of captives was brought to the city of Rome, where the slave-trade was a very flourishing business. They were brought from Angleland. These Angles had yellow hair, and fair skin.

As these captives, so different in looks from any one in Rome, were offered for sale, a good man passed by and saw them. It was a rich Roman senator, named Gregory, who had built six religious houses and then a seventh, in which he went to live himself, becoming its abbot. An abbot is the head of an abbey, or place of retreat where men are shut off from the world—they had many such in those days long ago. This abbot was so kind-hearted, and so anxious to help others, and really did so many good deeds, that he was called Gregory the Great. As this kind man passed the yellow-haired, fair-skinned captives, he was so pleased with their looks that he stopped to ask them some questions.

"Whence do you come?" said he.

"We are Angles," they answered, "from the

kingdom of Deira." This was then the name of what is now Yorkshire, England.

"God be gracious to you, my children," said the abbot kindly. "You are Angles? You are fair as angels. You should be Christians. I will go myself to your land and save your people from the wrath of God."

But the kind abbot's wish and purpose could not be carried out as far as going himself was concerned. He was not allowed to go. He was wanted at home. The pope died soon after, and Gregory the Great, as he was afterwards known, was the choice of all the people as the successor. He did not wish to be pope, and sent a letter to the emperor asking him to forbid the election, but somebody took the letter and never delivered it. Gregory was made pope. He cared neither for wealth nor authority, but now it was in his power to do more than before, and, although he could not go himself to the Angles, he could not forget them, and did not. The most important thing that he ever did in his life was to send missionaries to England. He sent a band of forty, with a leader from one of his abbeys. The missionaries went through France, and heard such dreadful things about the fierce ways of the Angles that they wrote back begging to be allowed to return home, but Gregory urged them on. In the year 597 they crossed over and set foot on the soil of distant England. But there was a Christian to meet them after all. Queen Bertha, wife of Ethelbert, was a daughter of the king of the Franks who had his throne in Paris, and she had learned of Jesus Christ. She remembered Him, even in the midst of all the heathenism about her, and went to pray in a little church that she had rebuilt. Though Ethelbert knew who Christians were, he knew very little about them, and was afraid to meet them anywhere but outdoors. He thought they would bewitch him with some spell, in the house, so met them under a tree.

Because the missionaries came from Rome, they were more respected, and their good lives spoke for them. They were given freedom to preach, and homes, and a church.

The king himself was converted, and afterwards ten thousand of his people in a day, put themselves on the side of Christ and the cross. The leader, Augustine, was made first Bishop of England, and the king gave him his own palace.

Surely it means much to us that so far back in history, the Gospel was carried to our ancestors. Let our thankfulness for this move us to send it on to others.

II

PATRICK
432-461 (In Ireland)

YOU all know when St. Patrick's Day comes in March, and for whom it was named. But did you ever know that he was a missionary to Ireland? When you look him up in history—where you really can find him, though some folk think he never actually lived, you will find him called just plain Patrick; but he was a good man, which was the principal thing.

Patrick, born late in the fourth century, in South-west England, as good authorities agree, was the son of a deacon, probably in the Evangelical British Church, and grandson of a presbyter, thus having Christian training.

When this boy was about sixteen, some wild Irish raiders came that way, plundering as they went, and took him as a slave, carrying him away to what is now known as Connaught. And a hard time he had of it as a swineherd, or keeper of pigs, for six long years.

But while in this sad condition of slavery, the youth began to think earnestly of his heavenly Father, and began to pray to Him. He often stole out before daylight to seek Him. At last he managed to escape from captivity, and found his way, in the midst of dangers, to the coast, where he found a vessel ready to sail. The crew was made up of heathen, and Patrick had a hard time to coax them to take him along. At last he succeeded, and always afterwards believed that it was in answer to his prayers to God. Part of the cargo consisted of Irish hounds, and the dogs were very fierce and hard to manage. Patrick seemed to have a great knack in handling animals, and the sailors were more reconciled to having him on board when they saw how well he could manage the cross dogs.

Three days of sailing brought the ship to France, but though Patrick wished to be rid of his present company, who were not pleasant companions, they did not seem to be in a hurry to part with him. Perhaps they wanted him to help with the dogs. At all events, they avoided the towns, and did not allow him to land very soon. By and by the young man found a quiet home in a little island in the Mediterranean Sea. It was a number of years before he got back to his English home.

Then he had a very wonderful dream, much like that which Missionary Paul had at Troas, when he saw that Macedonian who cried, " Come over and help us." It seemed to Patrick that a messenger stood by him, bringing letters from Ireland, containing a summons to that country where he had once been a slave, there to preach the Gospel of Jesus Christ. He was very sure that this was God's call to him to be a missionary, and was very anxious to obey. He went to France to study, and to enlist friends who would help him to go. He did not have an easy time of it, and it was fourteen years before he was finally sent to Ireland as a missionary. He seems to have begun his work there as a bishop.

From this time, for about twenty-nine years, till his death, March 17, 461, Patrick laboured in Ireland, except for one journey to Rome. He did many things, but gave most of his time to preaching to the heathen. From all that can be learned about him, he was a rare Christian, anxious to serve Jesus Christ, and full of enthusiasm. He carried the Gospel much farther than the power of Rome extended in Britain. He founded monasteries from which, later, others went, like Columba, as missionaries to western Scotland, northern England, to Italy and Germany, and even to far-off Iceland. When Patrick died, he was buried in the county of Down. His was a long and busy life, and after what he considered God's call, he never wavered in the belief that he was set apart to missionary work, nor in his earnest labours. A great many stories have been made up about this man that are like fairy tales, so that it is hard to believe that he was a real man. But there is enough history to prove that he *was* a real man and a missionary, and that he did a great deal of good in a time when heathenism and superstition placed many hindrances in the way of the work. Remember the truth about him, when next St. Patrick's Day comes round.

The above facts have been culled from a fuller history of Patrick in the book, "Great Men of the Christian Church," by Williston Walker, professor in Yale University, published 1908.

III

COLUMBA

The Latter Part of the Sixth Century

THE name of this stout missionary of the latter part of the sixth century ought to be remembered, for he did faithful work and did not spare himself. We are told that in his early life Columba was very fond of reading, of fighting, and of praying, and he seemed to find time to do a good deal of each; but the reading and praying belonged especially to the missionary part of his life.

Columba was the pioneer missionary in the north of Great Britain. In his time there were many churches in Ireland and Colum of the Kil (the cell or church), as his Irish name was, spent much time in visiting them. One of the first adventures told of this man was in connection with a book. He liked to read, but must have something to read. In those days one must buy, borrow, or copy a book if he wanted one. They had no printing-presses, you know, in those days. But in Ireland there were fine writers who could make beautiful copies of books, colouring the initials, and ornamenting the pages in a wonderful way.

Colum of the Kil had a neighbour, named Finnian, who had a gospel book which he copied with great pains and labour. He had to sit up nights after his day's work to do it. But when he wanted to take it home, Finnian said the book was his because copied from his. He called it "The Son-book" or the son of his book, and said "To every book belongs its son-book, as to a cow belongs its calf." Unfair as it was, Columba had to give up the copy he had made.

There were terribly bloody doings in Ireland in those times, and they say Columba helped in some of the fights, though at one time they said he prayed while his relations did the fighting. But finally the man left the warring country, and with a few friends set out to find a new home, sailing away in a little wicker boat. As long as they could see a glimpse of Ireland they would not land. Finally they came to the little island of Iona, only three miles wide in its widest part, and there the exiles landed. The island is off the west coast of Scotland. Somehow the wanderers got together a rude shelter, and a place to worship God. Then they began their voyages to the mainland round about. In the southern part of Scotland lived the Scots, and when Columba and his friends reached there, a new king had just begun to rule. Columba blessed and crowned this king, who had a rough sort of palace at Scone. It is said that the king sat on a big, rough stone to be crowned. When the English conquered Scotland, they brought this stone with them to London, where it is to this day. The Stone of Scone is in the Coronation Chair of England. You all know that, perhaps. You heard about it when King George was crowned. But perhaps you did not know that the first king crowned in Great Britain was blessed and crowned by Columba, a missionary of the sixth century.

All the missionaries who shared the work of Columba were trained at Iona, and from there went on their adventurous journeys. The men from Iona founded a mission station on another little island, off the east coast of England. They were not afraid of journeying, you see.

The Gospel was taken to Northumbria, and there the king called a conference of his chief men to talk over the new religion. One said that the gods of his fathers had done nothing for him, and he was willing to try a new God. Another, who must have been a sort of a poet, said, " Our life is like the flight of a bird through our lighted hall. In comes the bird out of the dark, flies about a little while in the light of our torches, and flies out again into the dark. So we come out of the dark, and go into the dark. If these strangers can tell us anything better, let us listen."

The principal one in all the missionary journeys was Columba. He was a great, big man, with stout arms, a broad chest, and a voice like the bellowing of an ox. He loved to send his little boat out into the fiercest storm. The ground was his bed, and his food was coarse. He carried his corn to mill on his own back, ground it, and brought it back again. He loved to study and to pray, though he was a good fighter, too. His heart was warm, and his people loved him.

By and by old age came on. One day he gave

his blessing to all those working under him, and, after looking over all the land, sat down to rest beside the barn while an old white horse came and laid his head against his breast. Then he went in. He had been copying the Psalms, and now came to the verse which was, as he wrote it : "They who seek the Lord shall want no manner of thing that is good." There he laid down his pen. He went into the little church, and was found kneeling there next morning, his work done.

IV

RAYMUND LULL
First Missionary to the Mohammedans (1290–1315)

YOU have heard of the Mohammedans, of course. Mohammed was the man who felt that he had received in visions a command to found a new religion. The principal thing that one had to believe was in this sentence: "There is one God and Mohammed is His prophet." Prayers five times a day, no matter where one might be, were to be offered regularly. The followers of this new prophet of a false religion were sent out everywhere to make converts, and they used the sword to make men believe. If one refused, he had his head cut off. There were soon a great many of these followers in the world, and you can see that they needed a missionary very much.

The Mohammedans got possession of the Holy Land, and it was to drive out these infidels that the Crusades were undertaken in the eleventh, twelfth and thirteenth centuries. The Crusades were the "armies of the cross," led by different kings and other leaders to the city of Jerusalem.

It was in this time of great events that Raymund Lull, the first missionary to the Mohammedan world, lived his life. He was born in 1235. Just count up now, and see how many years it is since this missionary was a new-born baby.

His birthplace was the Island of Majorca, off the east coast of what is now Spain, part of which was then called Aragon. When King James I of Aragon took this island from the Saracens, he gave large estates in it to the father of Raymund Lull, who had rendered his king distinguished service. The sovereigns of Aragon changed very often. Twenty proud kings reigned in a period of about four hundred years. The capital of the kingdom was Saragossa, and here, in the court, young Raymund Lull spent several years of his life, being court poet, and a skilled musician in the reign of James II. He had a rare mind and was an accomplished scholar, which gave him a high place among men. Besides this, he was heir to large wealth, and lived the life of a gay knight in the king's court before he became an ardent missionary.

He was thirty-two when the great change came, and his conversion seems to have been very much like that of Saul of Tarsus. It was in the city of Palma that the young man's whole life and aims were altered. At once he sold his property and gave all to the poor, except enough to support his wife and children in a simple way. Before long, he made up his mind to attack Mohammedanism or Islam, as it was called, not with the sword of steel but with the sword of Truth. He put on the dress of a beggar and went about among the churches of his native island, asking help for his work. In this, the thirteenth century, Islam had the greatest power in the world, and claimed more political influence and greater advances in science and poetry, than any of the nations. Against this mighty power Raymund Lull meant to lead the attack, using the weapons of love and learning only, not the force and fanaticism of the Crusades.

To accomplish his aim he began a thorough study of Arabic, the language of a large part of the oriental world. He also spent much time in meditation. He was about forty years old before he was ready to enter upon the life-work that he had planned as author and missionary, for he began to be a great writer. One of the first things he did at this time was to persuade King James II of Aragon to found and endow a monastery, where men should be taught the Arabic language, and should learn how to meet the Mohammedans in discussion, with learning equal to their own. Thirteen students were soon enrolled in this training school.

But Raymund Lull was not content. He longed for world-wide missions. He had spent some years in getting ready himself, and in helping the work at home. Now, at fifty-five, he decided to go alone to preach Christ in northern Africa. When he got to Tunis, he gave out the word widely that he was ready to debate with the Mohammedans, for he had studied both sides, and would answer whatever might be said. This was a great debate. The missionary proved the Truth, and some believed. But others were angry, and the missionary was thrown into prison, narrowly escaping death.

After great persecutions he got away to Europe, but he made other missionary journeys, and, fifteen

years after his banishment, was again on the shores
of northern Africa, in the stronghold of Mohammedanism. At the age of sixty-five he journeyed
through Cyprus, Syria, and other countries on his
missionary work. Returning to northern Africa
he stood up in a public place and proclaimed the
Truth, in Arabic, in the boldest way. Again he
was imprisoned, but some merchants took pity on
him, and finally he escaped with sentence of banishment. He was told that if he ever came back
he should die. He could not stay away, and came
back in 1314, quietly teaching, and praying with
converts, till his fiery zeal led him again to the
market-place to preach to those who had perse-
cuted him. He was seized and dragged out of town
where he was stoned to death, a brave martyr for
Christ, eighty years old.

He wrote one hundred and eighty books, established missionary colleges, and gave his life for the
Cause.

V

JOHN ELIOT

Apostle to the Indians (1645–1690)

COME, let us take a thought-journey back over two hundred and fifty years. Can you do it? Of course you can. You can think back thousands of years to the Flood, or

to the Garden of Eden, for that matter. You can *think* back much farther than you can *remember*.

Let us imagine that we are about eighteen miles southwest of Boston, on the Charles River, in the town with the Indian name, Natick. There seems to be something interesting going on in this little place, with woods around it. Look at the people coming together. Why—they are red men. Yes, they are Indians. Let us not be afraid of them. They are red, but they do not look fierce and wild. Now, see! A horseman is coming near. What a good face he has. He has come from Roxbury, we hear, where he has long been the pastor of a church. How kindly he greets the Indians. And now we hear what is to be done to-day. These

Indians are to be formed into a church of their own. It is the minister, Rev. John Eliot, of Roxbury, who has gathered the red men together. Every two weeks he comes to preach to them. In ten years we find that there are fifty of these "Praying Indians," as they are called.

Surely we wish to know something about the good man who has done so much for these children of the forest, who were in our land when the Pilgrims came.

John Eliot was born in England in 1604. The father died before the son was very far along in his education, and he left eight pounds a year to be used, for eight years, in keeping his boy at Cambridge University. After finishing at Cambridge, John Eliot taught school. He became a minister of the Church of England when he was twenty-seven years old, and soon after that came to America with three brothers and three sisters. Miss Hannah Mumford, to whom he was engaged, came the next year, and they were married—the first marriage to be put down in the records of Roxbury, Massachusetts. For sixty years this good minister was settled over Roxbury church.

But his heart yearned over the Indians. He believed that they had souls to be saved, and he felt that he must tell them of the Saviour. It was not easy to win them at first, but the minister was so kind and friendly that by and by the red men became devoted to him. Across the country he went, once a fortnight, as you know, riding on horseback to preach to his Indians. One after another he formed more settlements of Praying Indians. He taught them other things besides the Bible. He showed them how to raise crops, to build bridges, to make houses and homes, and how to clothe themselves properly. He made them comfortable, and by getting help from others, he made it possible for them to work, and to live as did their civilized brothers.

The red men had a government of their own among themselves, and it was wonderful how well they got on. Mr. Eliot was forty-one when he began to preach to them. In fourteen years there were thirty-six hundred Praying Indians. The government set apart six thousand acres of land for them.

After preaching a while, and explaining the Word of God, Mr. Eliot thought that these people ought to have the Bible in their own language. A very queer language it was, and hard to learn, but the good minister was not discouraged by that. He had the help of an Indian, taken captive in the Pequot War, in the work of translation. It was finished and printed in 1663, and was the very first Bible ever printed in America. Later, a revised version was printed at an expense of nine hundred pounds. Mr. Eliot gave towards this from his own small salary, the rest of the money coming from England. There are very few copies of this Indian Bible to be found now. One sold for five hundred and fifty pounds a while ago in England. Some words had to be supplied ; the Indians had no word for " salt," nor for " Amen."

Three years after the first printing of the Bible the busy missionary printed the grammar for the Indians. At the end of it he wrote this sentence which has become historic everywhere: "Prayer and pains, through faith in Jesus Christ, will do anything." Do you not wish to stop right here, and say that over, until you know it by heart? Please do. It will help you.

There are only fourteen or fifteen copies of the first edition of this grammar now to be found.

Mr. Eliot had a salary of only sixty pounds for his work in Roxbury and fifty for his Indian work, but he was one of the most generous men that ever lived. One time the treasurer, on giving him the money then due, tied it up in a handkerchief to keep him from giving away any of it. Visiting a poor family on the way home, and wishing to help them, the minister found the knots too hard to untie, and gave the kerchief to the mother, saying, "God must have meant it *all* for you."

He died in 1690, at the age of eighty-six, but is still unforgotten.

THOMAS MAYHEW

Who Began Missionary Work Among the Indians When
He Was Seventy (1658–1680)

SUCH a valiant soul ought surely to be in
cluded in the list of Heroes. Some folk
think their work is done at seventy, but not
so Mr. Thomas Mayhew, the New Englander,
Governor of Martha's Vineyard and adjacent
islands, in the far-back year of 1641. However,
his missionary work did not begin that year, and
it did begin first of all in the giving of his son to
devote his life to the Indians. Rev. Thomas Mayhew, Jr., was first a minister to the settlers in his
neighbourhood but extended his service of love to
the thousands of red men thereabouts.

His first accomplishment was the mastery of the
native language. He was very successful in this,
and soon had a flourishing mission. The first convert was named Hiacoomes. He put himself under
Mr. Mayhew's instruction, and became a teacher, and
afterwards a preacher to his own people. The very
first school in New England for the benefit of the
Indians was established in 1651. In another year
a church was organized. There were two hundred
and eighty-two members. The "covenant," which
all agreed to accept as church-members, was re-
pared in the Indian tongue by Mr. Mayhew.

About five years after this, the earnest missionary set out for England, to get money for his mission. He was lost at sea.

Then it was that his father, the governor, at the age of seventy, determined to take his son's place, and bravely began the study of the native language. Heroes are not all young men, you see, although many begin very early to be heroic.

This staunch missionary began preaching at the different plantations week by week in turn, sometimes walking twenty miles through the woods to meet his Indian congregations. In 1670 was organized the first Indian church with a native pastor. There were then about three thousand native Christians upon the island.

The indefatigable Mr. Mayhew kept on with his missionary work until he died, in his ninety-third year. Is not this a wonderful record?

His grandson, John, became associated with the work and was active in it until he died in 1688, when *his* son, Experience, took it up, and continued it for thirty-two years. In 1709 he translated the Psalms and John's Gospel.

Surely this is a family that should not be forgotten.

BARTHOLOMEW ZIEGENBALG
Missionary to India (1706-1719)

THIS missionary with the long name was once a baby no bigger than ordinary infants, but in the short life that he lived he made his name to be a shining memory in history.

He was born in June, 1683, in Pullsnitz, Saxony. He grew up in a Christian home, and early showed a talent for learning. He was sent to the University of Halle where he made a good record for talent, diligence, and Christian zeal.

Among the early helpers in mission work was King Frederick IV of Denmark, who became so earnest in his desires to help Christianize the world that, as one of the things in his power, he directed Professor Frank of Halle to choose two promising students from the university to go as missionaries to South India, in 1705. One of these was Bartholomew Ziegenbalg, and the other, Henry Plutsho. Both ready and eager to take up the mission.

After a long and wearisome voyage of many

34

months, they arrived at Tranquebar, a Danish possession on the coast of Hindustan. The governor kept them waiting for several days before consenting to see them, and then received them with great harshness. Ziegenbalg got a small room for himself in the Portuguese quarters, and began his missionary work under the greatest difficulties you can imagine. His comrade was gone elsewhere, the governor was opposed to him, and the European population of the city, engaged in money-making, cared nothing for missions. The idolatrous natives were ready to resist every effort to teach them a new religion. All these people wished nothing so much as to get rid of the missionary.

But this they could not do, since he was determined to stay. He had no grammar with which to learn the language, nor any dictionary to help him. At last he persuaded a native schoolmaster to bring his little school to the room where he lived that he might see how the children were taught. The scholars sat on the floor and made letters in the sand. The missionary sat down beside them, and imitated them till he knew the shape of all the characters that they made. Then he found a Brahman, one of the high caste men, who knew a little English, and by his help learned to speak the Tamil language in eight months. You must remember that there are many languages and dialects in India. The people do not all speak the same tongue, as Americans do.

The rajah finding out about the Brahman teacher, he was loaded with chains and cast into prison,

poor man. Some of the Europeans, in India for
getting gain, owned slaves. The missionary, pity
ing these poor creatures, and unable at once to find
others to teach, asked leave to teach these. He
was allowed to do it for two hours daily, and the
wretched outcasts came to him gladly. In less
than a year five slaves were baptized.

Missionary Ziegenbalg built a native church with
his own money, and at its dedication preached in
Tamil and in Portuguese to a congregation of
Christians, Hindus and Mohammedans. The second year he went about on extensive preaching
tours. In one place where there was a Dutch
magistrate, the most learned Brahmans were invited by him to hold a conference with the stranger. It lasted five days, and a great deal of truth
was given to them in this way.

In two years after reaching India, Ziegenbalg
had mastered the Tamil language so thoroughly
that he could speak it almost as readily as he could
his native German, and was ready to begin translations. He began to prepare a grammar and two
lexicons, one in prose and one in poetical form—a
great undertaking, this last, it seems to me. Tamil
prose would be hard enough, but to translate anything into Tamil poetry would be far harder. Yet
the missionary undertook it, because he thought it
wise, and in 1811 he finished translating the New
Testament into Tamil—the first translation of this
Book into any language spoken in India. He kept
on preaching to Hindus, slaves, Portuguese, and
even had a German service, largely attended. Be

sides the New Testament, he prepared a Danish Liturgy, German hymns, and a dictionary, with thirty-three other works, translated into Tamil. These were printed nine years after his arrival in India.

But now the missionary's health failed, and the next year he went home. He was able to go about telling his story of the far-off field, and it was a thrilling account. His glowing words impressed many in Germany and England, and kings, princes and prelates gave generously to the work, while crowds gathered to hear him.

In four years he returned to India, soon to finish his course. He died at thirty-six, after thirteen years of pioneer work in the period of modern missions. At his death there were three hundred and fifty converts, and a large number of cate-chumens, to mourn his loss and to carry on his noble work. His life had "answered life's great end."

VIII

DAVID BRAINERD
Missionary to the Indians at Twenty-four (1742–1747)

DO you know how it is possible to live a very long life in a very few years? Perhaps you have heard the secret told in these words: "He liveth long, who liveth well."

The young missionary to the Indians of long ago proved this to be true by his short, heroic, useful life.

In 1718 the little village of Haddam, Connecticut, was indeed a small one, but there, in April of that year, a baby was born who grew up into the man and the missionary that all who know anything of missions to-day, love to think about.

When David Brainerd was only nine, his father died, and five years later the death of his mother left him a lonely orphan. For a while he became a farmer's boy, and earned his living by his work out-of-doors. Then he went to live with a good minister, who gave him a chance to study, for the boy was very anxious to go to college. To Yale he went, while still quite young, and remained three years. There were no theological seminaries then, as now, to prepare young men to be ministers, but they studied with older ministers, and were made ready to preach in this way. Young Brainerd studied with different ministers, until the year 1742. Although he was then but twenty-four, he was considered ready to preach, and was sent out upon his chosen life-work as a missionary to the Indians.

At first, the intention was to send him to the tribes in New Jersey and Pennsylvania, but, because of some trouble among them there, the young missionary was sent instead to the Stockbridge Indians in Massachusetts.

Oh, but he had a hard time in the very beginning. You know, perhaps, that Solomon, the wise man, says that it is "good for a man to bear the yoke in his youth." It was certainly given to this young man to do this. No comfortable home was open to him, and he lived with a poor Scotchman, whose wife could hardly speak a word of English. Nothing better than a heap of straw laid upon some boards was provided for lodging, and as for food—what do you think he had ? We know exactly, for the missionary kept a journal, and in it he wrote—" My diet is hasty pudding (mush), boiled corn, bread baked in the ashes, and sometimes a little meat and butter." He adds, "I live in a log house without any floor. My work is exceedingly hard and difficult. I travel on foot a mile and a half the worst of ways, almost daily, and back again, for I live so far from my Indians." He writes that the presence of God is what he wants, and he longs to "endure hardness as a good soldier of Jesus." The Indians, from the first, seemed to be generally kind, and ready to listen, but, in the beginning, the work was slow.

The young missionary's heart was troubled for his poor red men, because the Dutch claimed their lands, and threatened to drive them off. They seemed to hate him because he tried to teach the Indians the way of life. At this time there was but a single person near with whom he could talk English. This person was a young Indian with eighteen letters in his last name, which was far enough from being " English." You may do your best at pronouncing it. It was " Wauwaumpequennaunt." Fortunately his first name was John !

The exposure and hardships of these days brought on illness from which the missionary suffered all through his brief life. He tells in his journal of spending a day in labour to get something for his horse to eat, after getting a horse, but it seems as if he had little use of it, for he was often without bread for days together, because unable to find his horse in the woods to go after it. He was so weak that he needed something besides boiled corn, but had to go or send, ten or fifteen miles, to get bread of any kind. If he got any considerable quantity at a time, it was often sour and moldy before he could eat it all.

He did not write complainingly of all this, but he did make a *joyful* entry one day, giving thanks to God for His great goodness, after he had been allowed to bestow in charitable uses, to supply great needs of others, a sum of over one hundred pounds New England money, in the course of fifteen months. It was truly, to him, " More blessed to give than to receive." He was thankful, he said, to be a steward to distribute what really belonged to God.

After two years' labour among the Stockbridge Indians, Mr. Brainerd went to New Jersey, his red brothers parting from him sorrowfully. The commissioners unexpectedly sent him to the Delaware Forks Indians. This meant that he must return to settle up affairs in Massachusetts and go back again to the new field. The long rides must be taken on horseback, the nights spent in the woods, wrapped in a greatcoat, and lying upon the ground. The missionary had flattering offers of pulpits in large churches where he would have had the comforts of life, but he steadfastly refused to leave his beloved Indians.

In the midst of difficulties and hardships he gladly toiled on. Travelling about as he did, he was often in peril of his life along the dangerous ways. On one trip to visit the Susquehanna Indians, the missionary's horse hung a leg over the rocks of the rough way, and fell under him. It was a narrow escape from death, but he was not hurt, though the poor horse's leg was broken, and, being thirty miles from any house, he had to kill the suffering animal and go the rest of the way on foot.

The last place of heroic service was in New Jersey, at a place called Crossweeksung. Here the missionary was gladly received, and spent two busy and fruitful years, preaching to the red men, visiting them in their wigwams, comforting and helping them in every way, being their beloved friend and counsellor at all times. At last he became so weak that he could not go on. A church and school being established, the way was made easier for another. Hoping to gain strength to return to his red brothers, David Brainerd went to New England for rest, and was received gladly into the home of Rev. Jonathan Edwards. Here he failed very rapidly, but his brave spirit was so full of joy that his face shone as with the light of heaven. He said, "My work is done." He died, October 9, 1747, at the age of twenty-nine. He opened the way for others to serve his Indians, and his life has helped many, and has sent others into the field through all these years since the young hero was called and crowned. The story of his life influenced William Carey, Samuel Marsden and Henry Martyn to become missionaries. Through these, David Brainerd spoke to India, to New Zealand and to Persia.

IX

WILLIAM CAREY

(" *The Consecrated Cobbler* ")

Missionary to India (*1793–1833*)

THERE was a young man long ago in England who asked some ministers if the Church had done all it could for the heathen, and received this answer: " Young man,  sit down. When God pleases to convert the heathen world, He will do it without your help or mine." Who was the venturesome young man ? William Carey.

Who was it that said afterwards, " Expect great things from God ; attempt great things for God " ? William Carey. Who was it that later said, when some one was talking of the great mine of heathenism, asking, " Who will go down ? " " I will, but remember that you must hold the ropes " ? William Carey, missionary to India for forty years. Tuck into your memory these three things, and keep them there, for they are worth remembering.

William Carey is called the father of modern missions. Of course we want to know something about him. In the year 1761, he was born in a lowly cottage, in the little town of Paulersbury in England. His father was a schoolmaster. In this village the boy spent the first fourteen years of his life, and his father gave him the best education he could. But at fourteen the boy was his own master. " The bench was his seat of literature, and the shoemaker's stall his hall of learning." The boy who, when but six years old, used to repeat sums in arithmetic to his mother, which he had worked out in his own mind, was not likely to stop learning at fourteen. He finished whatever he began. He used every chance he had. The room where he worked was filled with insects in every corner, and he delighted to watch them growing. He collected birds, butterflies, and animals, and was also fond of drawing and painting. He was an active fellow, and fond of the things boys love to do. He was a great favourite with those of his own age. As a shoemaker's apprentice, William Carey did his work so well that his master kept a pair of shoes to show William's good work.

While still a youth, he gave his heart to Christ, and was sometimes asked to speak in meetings in a little Baptist chapel which he attended. Thirty years afterwards, the minister who baptized the young man said, " In 1783 I baptized a poor journeyman shoemaker, little thinking that before nine years had passed he would prove the first instrument in forming a society for sending missionaries to the heathen, but such was the case."

At length the church encouraged the young

man to enter on the work of preaching, as he longed to do. But his master died, and the apprentice began work for himself to pay expenses while preaching. He married at twenty, and had his family to support. He preached three years at Barton, walking six miles there and back. Then he had a church in Moulton, where he had a salary of seventy-five dollars a year. He could not live on this—do you wonder?—and tried to teach school. This was a failure and he went back to shoemaking. But he and his family lived very sparingly, often going without meat for a month at a time. After two or three years he moved to Leister and built up a church there. All this time he managed somehow to do much studying. He mastered the Latin grammar in six weeks, and the Dutch language in a wonderfully short time. Greek and Hebrew were learned without a teacher. In seven years he could read his Bible in six languages. He bought a French book for a few pence and in three weeks could read it. He found it so easy to learn a new language that it was an amusement to spread out a book before him and study as he worked.

By and by the shoemaker preacher was asked to preach before an association of ministers. It was then and there that he said " Expect great things from God; attempt great things for God." As a result of that sermon, a Society for Propagating the Gospel among the Heathen was formed, in the little parlour of a lady named Mrs. Wallis. She loved to remember this, and her eyes glistened when it was mentioned.

Very soon Mr. Carey decided to go himself as a missionary. His wife felt that she could not go. There were four children, one of them a baby. The minister said he would take his oldest son and go, hoping the mother and the rest would follow. But before he sailed, the mother decided to go, and the whole family set out for India. It took five months for the voyage. On arriving, there were dreadful times and many hardships before a place could be found for the family, and Mr. Carey had to take what work he could get to support them. The money brought with them was gone, and the one trusted with it for the company of missionaries did not spend it wisely. Fifteen thousand miles from home, the only way to get more was to work for it. Mr. Carey said that he would not depend on the society at home, but would support himself, and sent for seeds and plants for a large garden. Soon after, the five-year-old son Robert died, and no one could be found to make or to carry the coffin. Men were afraid to touch the little body. Soon the missionary work began, though with many trials. After five years he went to Serampore, where his great work was done. After seven years in India, he baptized the first Hindu convert, who lived to preach for twenty years afterwards.

A wonderful work was done by the Mission Press. Before Dr. Carey died, 212,000 copies of the Scriptures had been sent out in forty different languages among three hundred millions of people.

After forty years' labour as missionary, professor, and translator, he fell asleep in Jesus.

X

THEODOSIUS VANDERKEMP

Who Went as a Missionary to Africa, When Past Fifty
Years Old (1799–1811)

IT is never too late to make a fresh beginning if Duty calls. This famous Hollander, who was born at Rotterdam in 1747, became eminent as scholar, soldier, and physician, before he

became the only medical missionary in Africa, at the beginning of the nineteenth century.

Dr. Vanderkemp's father was a minister of the Dutch Reformed Church. His son studied at the University of Leyden, and was well educated. He spent sixteen years in the army, where he was captain of horse, and lieutenant of dragoons —a valiant soldier.

Leaving the army, he went to Edinburgh. Here he became distinguished for his attainments in the modern languages and natural sciences. You can see that he was a very learned man. By and by he went back to Holland, and practiced medicine with great success. It seems that he could do many things well.

A great sorrow came to him in the death of his

47

wife and child in a shocking accident. This led to his becoming a Christian, and turning his thoughts to service for Jesus Christ. He offered himself as a missionary to the London Missionary Society for work in South Africa. He was ordained as a minister, and sailed in 1798, when past fifty. He went in a convict ship, and busied himself on the voyage in ministering to the spiritual and physical needs of the convicts.

After labouring in different places, and being ordered by the king to leave, with sixty followers, after establishing one station, Dr. Vanderkemp began special work for the Hottentots. In seven years those who gathered for worship numbered fully a thousand. The cruelties of the slave traffic so distressed the good doctor that, in three years, he paid $5,000 to redeem poor captives. Finally, by his efforts, aided by others, the Hottentots were made free. It was said that this missionary was wonderfully like the apostles of the early Church.

His service was not long, for he died in 1811, after only about twelve years in Africa. For a hundred years the Kaffir converts were called by his name.

Dr. Moffat said of this brave missionary: "He came from a university to teach the poor naked Hottentots and Kaffirs; from the society of nobles, to associate with the lowest of humanity; from stately mansions, to the hut of the greasy African; from the study of medicine to become a guide to the Balm of Gilead; . . . and from a life of earthly honour and ease, to perils of waters, of robbers, and of the heathen, in city and wilderness."

XI

JOHN ADAMS AND THE TRANSFORMED
ISLAND (*Pitcairn*)
1789–1829

NOW you shall hear a very wonderful story of what came about through one copy of the Bible and one man, in a tiny island in the Pacific Ocean.

The little speck of an island, but two and a quarter miles long, and one mile broad, is about 1,200 miles from Tahiti. This is a tale of the South Seas.

In the year 1767 (how long ago?) Captain Carteret, of Great Britain, was cruising round in those latitudes, and with him a young midshipman named Pitcairn. He was the first to discover the hitherto unknown island, and gave it his name. The poor young man died not long after. His naming of the island went down in the ship's log-book, and the next man who made a chart of the South Seas put a new dot on it for Pitcairn, and that was the last of this speck in the ocean for a long, long time.

Twenty years after, the good ship *Bounty*, flying the British flag, took her way homeward with plants of the breadfruit tree, which the government wished to introduce into the West Indies. Captain Bligh was in command. The master's mate was Fletcher Christian, a bright young man, but quick-tempered and revengeful. The captain was not as wise and kind as he might have been, and the mate was ready to resent everything, so that there was a bad state of feeling on board. At last Fletcher Christian, who was not well named, led the men in a mutiny. They overpowered the captain and his handful of faithful men, put them into a small boat loaded to the water's edge, within a few inches, and carrying a small allowance of provisions, and sent them adrift. It is dreadful to think of.

The mutineers then turned the vessel back to Tahiti, where they told a lie to account for their return, saying the captain had gone, with some of his crew, in another boat, with a friend, met on the sea. But the wicked men were in terror every moment, afraid they would be found out somehow and pursued to their death. They left the island, landed upon another, leaving some of the men behind, and taking some natives of Tahiti with them. They tried to build a barricade, but the work did not go well, and soon the *Bounty* was at sea again. Then was discovered the little island or Pitcairn, that seemed so solitary and forsaken that it promised safety. They landed and took up their residence there.

Let us imagine the scene. The men unload the ship and cast all her lading upon the shore. If we look carefully, we shall see an old Bible among the things tossed down. Now it is decided to "burr their bridges" by burning the ship, and soon the *Bounty* is a mass of flame, burning to the water's edge. Now these men must live with the savages brought with them, and see their English homes no more.

But shall we follow Captain Bligh and crew, set adrift nearly four thousand miles from any European settlement, with scanty supplies of food and water? They dare not land upon unknown islands for fear of being killed by savages. With two cocoanut shells for scales, and a leaden bullet for a weight, the captain daily measures and weighs the supplies for each man. Sometimes the storm-tossed boat quivers between waves "mountain-high" as the story-books say. Daily they pray for help, and God is good. At last they reach home, and tell their strange story. The ship *Pandora* scours the seas for the mutineers. Some are found at Tahiti but two have been murdered. Three are drowned on the homeward trip, the rest are punished with death on reaching England. But of Fletcher Christian and the rest not a trace is found.

The life in Pitcairn is very terrible. The men are in hourly dread of a visit from a man-of-war, and many a false alarm sends them scuttling to their hiding-places in the rocks. Fletcher Christian is so cruel that by and by the natives of Tahiti kill him and four other whites. Then the whites left, struggle with the natives, till all the Tahitan men are killed. It seems as if the tiny island runs blood. But time goes on. Children are born. A man who knows how to make an intoxicating drink from native plants brings this curse upon them.

At last one man only, of the crew of the *Bounty*

is left. He used to be called Alexander Smith but takes the name of John Adams. He taught himself to read, when a boy, from the signs and handbills on the London streets. One day he goes rummaging among the old things taken from the *Bounty*, and finds the Bible. Sick at heart over all the wickedness on the island, he reads God's Word. He prays. He finds and trusts God's promises. He gives his heart to God.

It is twenty-five years since the mutiny on the *Bounty*. Two men-of-war, one September evening, find an island not laid down in their charts. Next morning they see the homes of people on the shore —neat and comfortable they look. See. A canoe from the shore, with two young men, comes towards the ships, and hails them in the English tongue. How amazing ! They are taken on board and given some refreshments. Before they eat, they fold their hands and say earnestly, " For what we are about to receive, the Lord make us truly thankful."

By and by the story all comes out. John Adams has been the missionary who has taught those on the island to worship God and love His Word. It is this which has changed everything. He dies in 1829, forty years after the mutiny.

Another missionary goes out by and by, and the wonderful story goes on in the Transformed Island.

XII

HENRY MARTYN
Missionary to India and Persia (1806–1812)

SURELY it was a wonderful young missionary, who, dying at thirty-one, after only six years of service, left a name that has been remembered and loved for a hundred years. Wasn't his life worth living?

In the town of Truro, Cornwall, England, in 1781, lived a labouring man by the name of Martyn, who had risen to the place of chief clerk, in a merchant's establishment, by his own industry and business ability. Into this man's home came a baby boy who grew into a sensitive, proud, ambitious, and impetuous youth. He was so bright that he obtained a scholarship in St. Stephen's College, Cambridge. His only thoughts were of scholarship and fame, till his father's death made him think of higher things. When he was graduated with high honour, and seemed to have gained his highest ambition, he said that he found he had only grasped a shadow. He must find something better than self to live for. He had intended to be a lawyer, but finally felt called to the ministry, and then to the work of preaching to the heathen. Reading about William Carey's work in India turned his thoughts in this direction, but it was the life of David Brainerd which influenced him most. The story of this devoted life given to work among the North American Indians, fifty years before this, led Henry Martyn to become a missionary.

When he was but twenty-two, he offered himself to the Church Missionary Society to serve in India, and was accepted. But it was three years before he could go out. First he served as a curate in a village parish, in order to have better preparation for work abroad. And then he had to wait for a license. In those days no one could go from England to India without a license from the East India Company. The last trial which came to this young missionary about to set out was saying farewell to the lady he dearly loved, as he must do, if he went so far away. But he loved his Saviour so much that he gave up everything, even the one he loved best on earth, and sailed away, to see her no more. There was no other way.

The ship in which the young missionary sailed steered her course towards Africa. Then it was that the passengers learned, to their surprise, that there were soldiers aboard, who, at Capetown, attacked the helpless people there. Mr. Martyn was horrified, but as soon as he could, went ashore and ministered to the two hundred wounded men that he found in a wretched little hospital. At Capetown he met the old missionary Dr. Vanderkemp, and asked him if he had ever been sorry that he had left all to become a messenger to the heathen. " No," said the brave man, "and I would not exchange my work for a kingdom." Have you ever heard of a missionary who was sorry ? I never have. They seem to be the gladdest people anywhere.

Arrived in Calcutta, May, 1806, the young missionary wrote of the place that " the fiends of darkness seemed to sit in sullen repose in the land." It was very discouraging ; but the brave heart trusted God the more, and began the work of overturning the idols of the heathen. At Calcutta he made his home with a missionary named Rev. David Brown, who gave him a beautiful pagoda to live in. The English people of the city were so charmed with the refined manners, bright mind, and lovely spirit of Mr. Martyn that they wanted him to settle among them as a permanent minister, but his heart turned towards the millions in darkness. He got an appointment to Dinapore, whither he went to labour as almost the only one to stand up for Jesus in all the multitudes that swarmed about him.

It was as an English chaplain that he had been obliged to go out at first, not as a regular missionary, but he took this way in order to get a chance to do missionary work. He began to study Hindustanee diligently, and in two and a half years learned to speak it fluently. He began a school and afterwards established five. He began to translate the Bible, and to prepare tracts to give to the people. His native version of the New Testament was highly approved, but his Persic version, made for circulation among another set of people, was much injured by the malice of the interpreter, who put in words of his own choosing, which the common people could not understand.

A friend of those days writes of the missionary : "I perfectly remember the young man as he came into our home. He was dressed in white, and looked very pale. His expression was so luminous, intellectual, affectionate, and beaming with love, that no one thought of his features or form. Character outshone everything. There was also the most perfect manners, with attention to all minute civilities, and he was remarkable for ease and cheerfulness. He was the humblest of men."

While in Dinapore Mr. Martyn heard of the death of his two sisters at home from consumption, and the same disease began to show itself in him. He was ordered to Cawnpore, where he had a long illness. As soon as able to be out-of-doors, the missionary began his work again. He was so kind that he was soon known to a crowd of beggars who surrounded him when he went out. He arranged to have them come to him at a regular time once a week when he promised them each a small piece of money. In this way he gathered a company of about 500, who listened to his words after receiving his gifts. They were the lowest class and most wretched of the people. By and by he had to leave Cawnpore for his health, but went to Persia, there revising his Persic New Testament. Growing worse, he set out for England, but died suddenly at Tokat. several hundred miles from Constantinople.

XIII

GUIDO FRIDOLIN VERBECK

Who Received From the Japanese the Decoration of
The Rising Sun (1830–1899)

NOT all heroes are decorated by those governments whose people they seek to serve, but here is one who did receive that appreciation in Japan. You will keep on reading, I am very sure, until you find out how it was.

You will guess at once from this good man's name that he was not an American, or, at least, that his parents were not. He was born in Utrecht, the Netherlands, in 1830, but in his young manhood he sailed from New York, in 1859, for Japan, as a missionary from The Reformed Church in America. He set forth in May, and in November he reached Nagasaki, Japan. It took longer then than it does now.

For nearly forty years this missionary was an influence in this country, and had an active part in the progress of Protestant missions there.

Do any of you remember the story of the conversion of a Japanese officer through finding a

floating Testament on the water? There was
such a man, "really and truly," and his name was
Wakasa. He was commander-in-chief of Japanese
forces at Nagasaki. One day he noticed something floating on the waves, and sent some one to
bring it to him. It proved to be a copy of the
New Testament, in English. The officer was very
curious about it, and after many difficulties got
some one to read it to him. He came in contact
with Dr. Verbeck, and in 1866 was baptized by
him, as a Christian, through the study of God's
Word.

Perhaps you know that the "Two-sworded
Class," having a right to carry two swords, is one of
very high rank in Japan. Dr. Verbeck taught
two classes of Two-sworded young men, in Nagasaki, at one time.

In 1868, when the Revolution in Japan broke
out, these young men remembered their instructor,
of whom they thought highly, and as they were
now prominent in government affairs, they sought
out the missionary and asked his advice about fram-
ing their new institutions—a great honour indeed to
pay to a foreigner.

The advice given was so good and acceptable
that the adviser was called to Tokyo. There he
stayed for nine years, in close connection with the
government, helping to shape it, and supervising the
university, and the system of education which was
the first established. The first deputation of Japanese that went on a tour among the nations of
Europe took Dr. Verbeck along.

In recognition of his services in this and other directions he was decorated by the government as one of the third class of The Rising Sun, and was thus entitled to appear at court. In translating, teaching, preaching, and living, he was a power, for forty years, in planting Christianity in the Sunrise Kingdom.

Later, Dr. J. C. Hepburn, first medical missionary from America to Japan (1815), had the decoration sent him on his ninetieth birthday, at home, by the Emperor of Japan.

XIV

ALEXANDER DUFF
Missionary to India (1830–1864)

ALEXANDER DUFF was another bright boy who began early to prepare for a useful life. He was a Scotch laddie, born in Perthshire, in 1806. At fifteen he entered the University of St. Andrew. He grew to young manhood during the time of a great awakening in the interest of missions all through Scotland. Having become an earnest Christian, he heard the call to preach the Good News to the heathen, and when he was twenty-three he was sent as a missionary to India. The voyage was anything but safe and easy. Twice he nearly lost his life in a wreck; first on a rocky reef when rounding the Cape of Good Hope, and again on the coast of Ceylon. A third time he barely escaped with his life in a wreck near the mouth of the Ganges River. In the first wreck the missionary and his wife lost everything, not even saving a book from their library, nor any of the precious plans and manuscripts they carried. It took them eight months to reach Calcutta. Were they discouraged? Not at all.

The chief thing that young Mr. Duff intended to do was to open a school which would give a good education to Hindu youths. The language was to be English, so that the missionary teachers would not have to learn a foreign tongue. The Bible was to be regularly taught every day. The Orientals wanted all instruction to be given in Sanskrit, but they could not bring it about. The missionary had his way, and did what he came out to do. How many students came the first day, do you think? Five. And where did the school open? Under a banyan tree. There was no other place, and this did very well. Before the first week ended there were three hundred applications, and very soon there was a good building provided for the two hundred and fifty accepted pupils. They learned English readily, and studied the Bible every day. By and by the natives began to feel that it was the Bible which made the English people different from themselves. They saw the kindness of the missionaries, and wondered over their leaving home to try to help others far away. They asked, "What makes them do all this for us?" and then they answered, "It is the Bible."

The second year, three times as many students came, and before very long the number increased to a thousand. Wasn't that grand progress? And many became Christians, and faithful ones, too, which was best of all. The story of one of the converts is very touching. A man came to one of the missionaries and told him that he wanted leave to die in his house. He showed in his worn face that he was near death. He was about sixty years old, and had been a Christian for twenty years. But he had "lost caste" by this, and was cast out by those of his own class and family. No one would have anything to do with him. All these years he had lived alone, and had been faithful to his Master. Now he was sure that the end was near, and longed to die in the house of a Christian missionary. He was kindly cared for through five weeks of suffering, and then his pain and loneliness were over. Before he died, the missionary said to him one day, "Captain (for he had been in the army), how is it with you?" The man's thin face kindled into a beautiful glow as he said, "Jesus has taken all mine and given me all His." The missionary asked, "What do you mean by 'all mine'?" "All my guilt, all my sin," said the man. "And what is 'all His'?" asked his friend. "All His righteousness, all His peace," and then he fell asleep—triumphant in Jesus.

In 1834 Dr. Duff, as he was then, went back home. He was in such poor health that he could not stay longer in India without a vacation. But he spent the time at home, as far as he possibly could, in going about and stirring up the people with his burning words, as he told of the great work abroad. He was asked to become the principal and professor of theology in the Free Church of Scotland, and urged strongly to accept. But he could not and would not, begging them to allow him to remain always a missionary to the heathen.

Returning to India, and then after a time returning to Scotland, he had many honours bestowed upon him.

In 1857 the earnest missionary went back to India after having spoken to thousands upon the mission work. This time he opened a school for high caste girls, that is, girls of the highest class. There were sixty-two enrolled the first year. When examination day came at the close of the year, many high caste gentlemen of India came to the exercises, and said they were very much pleased with all that they saw and heard. It used to be said in that land that one might as well try to teach a cow as to teach a girl anything, but the girls showed that they could learn when they had a chance.

At last Dr. Duff's health failed utterly and he had to leave the field. For fourteen years he helped the Cause in the home-land, and passed away in peace, at the age of seventy-two.

XV

CAPTAIN ALLEN GARDINER
The Man Who Wanted "a Hard Job" (1834–1851)

LOOK at your map for Patagonia and Terra del Fuego, at the southernmost point of South America. The people there used to be among the very worst known anywhere. They

were cannibals, and the filthiest of creatures, besides being the cruelest. When they talked it sounded like a man clearing his throat, and it was almost impossible to understand them. They believed that a good spirit lived in the sun and two bad ones in the moon, and that good people, at death, went to the sun, and bad ones to the moon. You can imagine what a hard thing it would be to try to Christianize such people. There was a young man, long ago, who said he wanted to be sent to the hardest place to do the hardest missionary work that needed to be done. He did not ask or seek easy work, and took the hardest. It was Captain Allen Gardiner.

This brave hero was born in England in 1794. When a boy he loved the water, and was trained in

64

the English Naval College, afterwards becoming a captain. In his voyages he went to China. Seeing the Chinese engaged in dreadful idol-worship made him long to help them, and others like them. He gave his heart to Christ, and, while still a voyager, got leave of absence from his ship as often as possible, and went into the interior to find out the condition of the natives of foreign lands. In this way he became interested in the wild natives of the mountains in and about Patagonia. He was now a man of thirty, filled with a desire to be a missionary. The London Society could not answer his appeals. Ten years passed. His parents died, and also his young wife. He had a small income, and decided to send himself, if the Society could not send him to a foreign field.

He and a Polish companion went first to Africa, and began a mission among the Zulus—preaching through an interpreter, and teaching the children to read and to wear clothes. After three years Captain Gardiner visited England and returned with a band of missionaries, but war between Zulus and Boers broke up the mission.

The captain could not give up his hope to labour among the heathen. He went to South America and travelled about for two years, deciding to begin work in New Guinea, but the Dutch would not allow it, distrusting him because he was an officer in the Royal Navy of England. Then he decided to make Terra del Fuego his field. The savage inhabitants would not make friends with him. He went back to England and tried in vain to arouse

interest in these benighted people. But he got a
grant of Bibles and New Testaments and went
about distributing them. Going again to England
he failed once more in arousing interest, but finally
some friends formed a committee for carrying on
the Patagonian mission, and sent out Robert Hunt
as a catechist. Captain Gardiner went with him at
his own expense. Alas! The natives had moved.
All search for them was vain. No Indians were
to be found. After a while the chief and a few
others returned, but in such a surly mood that nothing could be done but leave the station. An English
ship passing that way took them home.

Do you think the brave missionary was discouraged now? Not a bit of it. He felt that those
degraded Indians needed Jesus, and he was more
anxious than ever to preach Christ to them. In
1848 he started again, travelled about among the
natives, returning to England to beg for help for
them. He was allowed to go back with a ship-car-
penter and four sailors. After great trouble they
landed, but the natives were so dishonest that it was
found best to try to have the mission afloat. Captain Gardiner again returned to get better equipment.

Again he was met with indifference, but at last,
a thousand pounds being raised, of which he gave
three hundred himself, back he went. His soul was
stirred by a perfect passion to lead those savages
to Jesus Christ. Six others went with him on this
voyage. They carried six months' provisions and
arranged for supplies for six months more to be

sent, sailing for Picton Island. But no vessel would stop there with the second supply, and the stores were sent to the Falkland Islands. The governor tried to forward them, but in vain. The little party of missionaries was left destitute, and at the mercy of the pitiless Fuegians, with only shell-fish, wild celery and seaweed to eat, drinking rain water from the hollows in the rocks. At last a ship was sent out in search of the brave men, and it was found that they had starved to death. The bodies were found, and the writings they had left, including Captain Gardiner's journal.

One of the dauntless men, Mr. Williams, wrote that though his body was weak, his spirit was strong and glad, and that he would not change situations with any man living. He felt that he was in the path of duty, even when death drew near. It was all very sad, and it looked as if the mission of Captain Gardiner had failed. But no. The story of his valiant effort was spread far and wide, and his death did what his life could not do—it made men say, "With God's help the mission shall be maintained." And it was. Others went out. Native boys were brought back to be educated. A ship, the *Allen Gardiner*, took out missionaries. Some were murdered, but others went. At last the work prospered, and many fierce natives were won to Jesus Christ.

XVl

CYRUS HAMLIN

*Founder of Robert College, Missionary in Constantinople
for Thirty-four Years (1839–1873)*

A MAN that founds a college is worth know
ing. Don't you think so? Let us get
acquainted, then, with Cyrus Hamlin, who
was the founder of Robert College in Constantinople,

and a teacher, scholar,
missionary, inventor, ad-
ministrator, and states-
man. Hannibal Ham-
lin, Vice-President of
the United States dur-
ing the administration
of President Lincoln,
was first cousin to this
missionary.

Cyrus Hamlin was born on a farm near Water-
ford, Maine, January 5, 1811. When the baby was
only seven months old, the good father died, leaving the mother to struggle hard to bring up her
children. When he was but six, the boy began his
education under a teacher in a little red school-
house. As he grew older, the books read in the
home were much like those that Lincoln read—
Goldsmith's "History of Greece and Rome," "Pilgrim's Progress," "Vicar of Wakefield," and Rollin's

"Ancient History." The Bible was always read, and the *Missionary Herald*.

One of the first things the boy undertook to make was an ox-yoke, which was made from yellow birch wood, and was called "a thing of beauty." Afterwards he made almost every tool and article needed on the farm, though he had no teacher.

When Cyrus was eleven, he was allowed to go to town on Muster Day, a great holiday in those times, when they had sham fights with Indians, and parades, such as boys like. His mother gave him seven cents to buy gingerbread, but said as she gave it, "Perhaps you will stop at Mrs. Farrar's and put a cent or two in the contribution box." The boy tried to divide the seven cents in his mind, before he reached Mrs. Farrar's, but could not satisfy himself as to how many he would give, and how many he would keep. When he reached the house he said to himself, "I'll just dump them all in." And so he did, and went without gingerbread. Returning home hungry as a bear, he said that he had had nothing to eat, and his mother gave him a bowl of bread and milk. He said it was the best he had ever eaten.

When he was sixteen, Cyrus began to learn the trade of a silversmith in Portland, and in three years developed the mechanical skill for which he was afterwards famous. At seventeen he united with the church, and joined a society of Christian young people, though in those days there were no Christian Endeavour organizations. One day a good deacon who had watched the young Christian

asked him if he did not think he ought to be a minister. The answer was that the expense would be
too great. The deacon said that the church had
voted to give a thousand dollars for such use, and
this decided the matter. The eager student began
his preparation, first in school, then in Bowdoin
College, where the poet Henry W. Longfellow was
among his classmates.

In the winter of 1831, in Bowdoin College, two
young men, preparing to be missionaries, had a
great influence upon some of the students. Cyrus
Hamlin was one of those who volunteered for the
foreign field. When he told his mother, she said,
" Cyrus, I have always expected it, and I have not
a word to say."

One day the professor lectured on the steam
engine in the college class, and it appeared that
but few had ever seen one. Young Hamlin said,
" I think I could make one so that any one could
understand its parts." " I wish you would try it,"
said the professor. The young man resolved to
" do it or die." He succeeded, and the work of
three months brought him $175.00 for his model.
It is now in the cabinet in the college.

Bangor Theological Seminary received this
bright student after he had been graduated from
college with highest honours. At last he was ready
for his work abroad, and was appointed to Turkey.
Miss Henrietta Jackson, who was a young lady
well adapted to be his helper, consented to go with
him as his bride.

The second day after landing in Constantinople

the two young missionaries began to study the language. It was a troublous time in the land, and there were many hindrances to mission work. It was a year before a school could be opened and then it began with but two pupils. Before long there were twelve.

Mr. Hamlin fitted up the school with all sorts of appliances, which he was skilled in making. The Orientals thought such work was done by Satan, but flocked to see the appliances, and to watch experiments in the laboratory, often staying to ask about the Christian religion.

The missionary, now Dr. Hamlin, gave much help to students through his workshop. His next enterprise was to establish a bakery in connection with a mill. This not only helped the poor Armenians wonderfully, but when the Crimean War broke out, the bakery supplied bread for the hospital where Florence Nightingale laboured, and also for the English camp. Dr. Hamlin built more ovens, and agreed to furnish from twelve to twenty thousand pounds of bread daily. Seeing how the sick and wounded soldiers suffered for want of clean clothes this dauntless missionary, who believed in helping in every possible way, invented a washing machine, which was the greatest boon. With six machines and thirty persons, 3,000 articles could be washed in a day. Dr. Hamlin said that he had been credited with sixteen professions but that of washer-woman was the one that he was most proud of.

In 1860 began the great work of founding Robert College in Constantinople. It was named for Dr. Hamlin's friend, Mr. Robert, who aided the work.

There were more difficulties in the way than you could count. It was hard to get permission to buy a site, and to build. The money had to be raised in America in the time of the Civil War. The college opened with four students, but soon had forty. Dr. Hamlin finally finished his busy life, in the home-land, in 1900.

XVII

ROBERT MOFFAT
Missionary to South Africa (1817–1870)

IS it not wonderful to think of doing one thing for over fifty-three years? That was keeping at it faithfully, indeed. Robert Moffat was a hero-missionary in South Africa for as long a  time as this, and never once said he was tired of it and would give it up.

This brave missionary came into the world December 21, 1795, in a little town in Scotland. His parents were poor in this world's goods, but rich in having seven children, and they were sturdy, honest, good people.

When the little Robert began to go to school he had no text-book but the Westminster Shorter Catechism, with the alphabet on the title-page. He did not care very much about study, and the master sometimes tried to help him with his rod. When he grew older, he longed for " a life on the ocean wave " and ran away to sea. He had some hard times, and several narrow escapes, which made him glad to give up a sailor's life. He then at tended a school which pleased him better than the first one, and studied bookkeeping, astronomy, geography, and mathematics. It was well that he gave his mind to these studies then, for in six months his school days ended. At fourteen the boy became self-supporting, being set to learn gardening.

Robert's mother, good, earnest Christian Scotch-woman that she was, did a great deal for her son. She was very much interested in missions, and it was from her lips that he first heard about the heathen, and the work of helping them. The mother talked cheerfully and wisely to her children, as they sat about the fire in the evenings, all knitting busily. The boys as well as the girls used to knit in those days. What do you think of that? Certainly it was a useful thing to do.

The gardener, to whom Robert was apprenticed, was a hard master, and it was then, when it was so hard to get, that the boy began to long for a better education. He joined an evening class and began to study Latin and geometry. He also learned to use blacksmith's tools at this time, and how to play on the violin. His music was a great comfort to him long afterwards, and everything he learned was of use to him as a missionary. At sixteen he went to England. His mother asked him to promise to read the Bible every day. He gave his word and kept it. In England Robert the gardener found a good place, and his master, seeing that he was anxious to learn, encouraged and helped him to study. Not long after beginning the life in

England, the young man was invited to some special meetings and gave his heart to the Saviour. He was so happy that he wanted to tell everybody, and then an intense longing came into his heart to carry the news to the heathen. But he was not yet fitted to be a missionary and the London Missionary Society refused to send him. But one of the officers became interested in him, and advised him to come to Manchester, and study under his care. A Mr. Smith, who was much interested in missions, gave the young man a place in his nursery garden. It was a very good place, and more than that, gave him a chance to know Miss Mary Smith, who afterwards became his devoted and helpful wife.

By and by Mr. Moffat was accepted by the Missionary Society and began to prepare for his life as a missionary. When the time came, he had to go alone to Africa, as Miss Mary Smith's parents felt that they could not give up their bright young daughter, though she was willing to go as the missionary's bride to the dark land so far away. Mr. Moffat set forth on his lonely way. Arrived in Africa, he had all sorts of trials and dreadful experiences for more than a year before he reached the station in Namaqualand, known as Afrikaner's Kraal, north of the Orange River. Afrikaner had been a fierce and cruel chief, but some missionaries had led him to Christ. He now welcomed Mr. Moffat and said he must stay. He bade the women bring materials for a kraal, or house of poles and mats, plastered with mud, and shaped a little like a beehive. In half an hour the kraal was finished, and the missionary lived in it six months, though it was not very comfortable to have the hungry dogs running in and out, and snakes dropping down at any time.

One of the first things Mr. Moffat taught the people was to wash themselves and put on decent clothing, while he told them of Jesus who would take away their sins. The chief gave him two cows which saved him often from going hungry to bed, as his salary was not quite $120.00 a year and how could he get everything needful with that sum?

After two years and a half, Miss Smith's parents consented to her going to Africa, and after a long voyage of several months she arrived, and was married to the good missionary. The two opened many stations, and did their work under the greatest difficulties that you can imagine. It was very hard to learn the language, for it was not written and there were no books. The interpreters took pleasure in telling them the wrong words, which made it harder. At last Mr. Moffat was able to write a spelling book and have it printed in England, afterwards writing a catechism, and translating parts of the Bible. Nine years passed before there were any great signs of success, but then there was a wonderful awakening among the Africans, and a new church had to be built to hold the converts, while the sound of praise and prayer came from many homes. After twenty-three years of service, Mr. Moffat took his wife and returned home for a visit. After telling his story, and receiving great honours, he went back with Mrs. Moffat to the work they both loved. After thirty years more, they returned to England The next year Mrs. Moffat died, and twelve years later, aged eighty-seven, the husband followed. He who once said, " I have sometimes seen in the morning sun the smoke of a thousand villages where no missionary has ever been," went to many of them with the true light that still shines.

XVIII

SAMUEL J. MILLS

The Missionary Who Never Reached His Field
(Died in 1818)

PERHAPS you know that near Williams College, Williamstown, there is, this very day, a monument in the shape of a haystack, as a reminder of what took place once upon a time, under a real haystack, on this spot. Very early in the nineteenth century, somewhere about 1809–10, there were four young men in Williams College who used to meet together in a grove for prayer and conference. One day a heavy shower forced them to find better shelter than the trees afforded, and they took refuge under a haystack in a field near by. They were earnestly talking on this day about sending the Good News to the far-away heathen, and in the shelter of that haystack they pledged themselves to go as foreign missionaries as soon as the way should open. The best known of these four students was Samuel J. Mills, born in Massachusetts, in the town of Tolland, and now about twenty-five or twenty-six years old.

At this time, Mr. Mills, with the other three, came to Andover to enter the theological seminary there. Here they met young Adoniram Judson, who was just then looking for some way to be sent to the foreign field. But there was no Society or Board ready to send anybody to heathen lands. There was the Massachusetts Missionary Society, which was founded in 1799, but its work was limited to the North American Indians, and it could do nothing for these young men who wished to go to India, Burma, and Africa. At last, after talking over matters, and asking advice of others, besides making it a subject of earnest prayer, a paper was drawn up, telling their wishes, and asking support, direction and prayers from the ministers who were gathered at the time in what was called The General Association.

At first there were six names signed to this document, but, for fear the ministers might be alarmed at the thought of providing for so many, two names were taken off, one of them being that of young Mr. Judson. The assembled ministers adopted a set of resolutions in their meeting, which finally led to the organization of a new Society, or Board, called The American Board of Commissioners for Foreign Missions, which, in due time, set apart the young ministers to be missionaries to go to far-off heathen lands.

Samuel J. Mills, who was the son of a minister, now began to look forward to a work in foreign countries, such as his heart had long been set upon. But after his graduation day, there seemed to be a great deal for him to do first in the home-land. He had been one of those whose petition had been, in part, the means of organizing a new Society to send out missionaries. Now he helped to start the

Bible Society, which was as important as any
Mission Board. Unless there were Bibles to take,
and in the language of the heathen, how could
messengers take them to those who had never heard
the Word ? So the Bible Society was formed.

The work of Home Missions used to be called
Domestic Missions, and every one knew that this
must be carried on too, and Mr. Mills did much to
help in the work at home. Then he helped to
organize another Foreign Mission Board called The
United Foreign Missionary Society. Next came
the African School, under the care of the Synod of
New York and New Jersey, and Mr. Mills had his
share in planning this work for the coloured people.
The American Colonization Society, which planned
to send out colonies to other lands, now chose Mr.
Mills to go as their messenger to Africa, and to
choose a good place to send a colony, or company
of negroes from America, to live in a land from
which the first black people came. Mr. Mills had
been a helper in getting this Society started, and
now, at last, he was to go to the foreign field himself, and, in this way, make a beginning in missionary work.

Joyfully he set sail in a ship, but before he could
carry out his mission, he was taken ill with fever.
He was not very strong and the dread disease ran
its course. The young missionary-to-be died on
shipboard, in strange waters, on the 16th of June,
1818. He was only thirty-five years old, and had
not been able to carry out the great wish of his
life ; but, after all, he did much for the heather

world in the organization of the societies that carried on the work he loved, and longed to share. Besides, this young missionary-to-be was so good—so earnest, loving, faithful, and enthusiastic, that others caught his interest in missions. Even to-day, when over ninety years have passed since his life's service ended on that ship in far-off seas, people are better for knowing the life, and hearing the story, of Samuel J. Mills, remembered still for the work he did.

XIX

ADONIRAM JUDSON
Missionary to Burma (1813–1850)

A DARK-EYED baby boy lay in his old-fashioned cradle more than one hundred and twenty-four years ago. In the little town of Malden, Massachusetts, August 9, 1788, this child was born, and named Adoniram, after his father, who was Rev. Adoniram Judson, a Congregational minister in that far-away time. The father, and the mother, too, thought this baby a wonderful child, and determined that he should do a great deal of good in the world. They thought that the best way to get him ready for a great work was to begin early to teach him as much as he could possibly learn. Long pieces were given him to commit to memory when he was hardly more than a baby, and he learned to read when he was three. Think of it!

When he was four, he liked best of all to gather all the children in the neighbourhood about him and play church. He always preached the sermon himself, and his favourite hymn was, "Go, preach My Gospel, saith the Lord." This was a good way to have a happy time, and he wasn't a bit too young to think about telling others the Good News, for he was old enough to know about Jesus and His love.

The little Adoniram, like boys who live now, liked to find out about things himself. When he was seven, he thought he would see if the sun moved. For a long time he lay flat on his back in the morning sunlight, looking up to the sky through a hole in his hat. He was away from home so long that he was missed, and his sister discovered him, with his swollen eyes nearly blinded by the light. He told her that he had "found out about the sun's moving," but did not explain how he knew.

At ten this boy studied Latin and Greek, and at sixteen he went to Brown University, from which he was graduated, as valedictorian of his class, when he was nineteen. He was a great student, loving study, and ambitious to do and be something very grand and great indeed. Two years after this, he became a Christian, and then came a great longing to be a minister, and he studied diligently with this end in view. There was one question which this splendid young man asked about everything, and this was, "Is it pleasing to God?" He put this question in several places in his room so that he would be sure to see and remember it.

Mr. Judson taught school for a while, wrote some school-books, and travelled about to see the world. After some years he read a little book called "The

Star in the East." It was a missionary book, and
turned the young man's thoughts to missions. At
last he seemed to hear a voice saying, "Go ye,"
and with all his heart he said, "I will go." From
that moment he never once faltered in his determination to be a missionary. His thoughts turned
towards Burma, and he longed to go there. About
this time Mr. Judson met the four young men who
had held a prayer-meeting in the rain, when they
sheltered themselves in a haystack, and there promised God to serve Him as missionaries if He would
send them out. These five were of one heart, and
were much together encouraging one another.
There was no money to send out missionaries, and
Mr. Judson was sent to London to see if the Society
there would promise some support. The ship was
captured by a privateer, and the young man made
prisoner, but he found an American who got him
out of the filthy cell. This man came in, wearing
a large cloak, and was allowed to go into the cell
to see if he knew any of the prisoners. When he
came to Mr. Judson he threw his cape over him,
hiding him from the jailer, and got him out safely,
giving him a piece of money, and sending him on
his way. The London Society was not ready to
take up the support of American missionaries, but
not long after this, the American Board, in Boston,
sent him to Burma, with his lovely young bride,
whose name, as a girl, was Ann Hasseltine. It took
a year and a half to reach the field in Rangoon,
Burma, and get finally settled, in a poor, forlorn
house, ready to study the language. By this time,

Mr. Judson was taken under the care of the Baptist Board, just organized, as he felt that he belonged there. The Burmans were sad heathen, and the fierce governors of the people were called " Eaters." The work was very hard, but the missionary said that the prospects were " bright as the promises of God." When he was thirty-one and had been in Burma six years, he baptized the first convert to Christianity. The preparation of a dictionary, and the translation of the New Testament, now occupied much time.

After this came great trouble. It was war time. Missionaries were unwelcome. Dr. Judson was put in a dreadful prison. After great suffering there, his wife was allowed to take him to a lion's cage, left empty by the lion's death. She put the translation of the New Testament in a case, and it was used for a pillow. After he left the prison, a servant of Dr. Judson's found and preserved the precious book. Set free at last, he went on with his work. Death came to his home again and again, and trials bitter to bear. For thirty-seven years he toiled on, several times returning to America, but hastening back to his field. By that time there were sixty-three churches in Burma, under the care of one hundred and sixty-three missionaries and helpers, and over seven thousand converts had been baptized. Worn out with long labour, the hero-missionary, stricken with fever, was sent home, only to die on shipboard, and his body was buried at sea.

XX

THE THREE MRS. JUDSONS
Helpmeets to the Missionary in Burma

Miss Ann Hasseltine

THERE was a pleasant stir in the little village of Bradford, Mass., one day, in the year 1810. It was the occasion of a meeting of the Missionary Society, or General

Association of Massachusetts, and the delegates were entertained with great hospitality. A number of these worthies, older and younger, were gathered at the table of a Mr. Hasseltine for dinner, and among them young Mr. Adoniram Judson, who had just signified his great desire to go as a missionary. Pretty Ann Hasseltine waited on the table. A gifted and sprightly girl she was, as well as beautiful and good. She looked with curious interest upon the young man whose bold missionary projects had made a stir in the meeting, but to her mind, he was wholly absorbed in his plate. How could she guess that he was that very moment engaged in composing a graceful bit of verse in her praise? Yet so it was, and he must have found courage to tell her this, and other things, by and by, for she afterwards went to Burma as the wife of the bold missionary. At that time it was India that was the chosen field.

Ann Hasseltine was born in Bradford, Mass., in 1789. She was a restless, merry, vivacious girl, richly gifted. At sixteen she entered the service of her Saviour with all her heart, and her brightness and beauty became His. She taught school for some time after leaving Bradford Academy, which gave her added fitness for the life of a missionary, which she entered, in 1812, on her marriage to Mr. Judson, afterwards Dr. Judson. She was one of the very first lady-missionaries. The *first* from America was Mrs. Kaske, going with her husband in 1746 to South America.

The two missionaries had a serious time reaching their field. The East India Company decided that missionaries were not desirable, and ordered them back to America, but finally allowed them to go to the Isle of France. They then planned to go to Madras, but the East India Company had jurisdiction there, and finally, the only way that opened was to Rangoon, Burma, a place always held in great dread. But they embarked for Rangoon in a crazy old vessel, and were tossed about so violently that Mrs. Judson was dangerously ill. She recovered after landing. Everything was forlorn and gloomy enough, but they took courage and set about their work.

Mrs. Judson learned the language very quickly, and used it to advantage. Four years after setting out upon the voyage to Burma, little Roger Williams, who had for eight months been the joy of the missionary home, was taken from them.

Twice Mrs. Judson had to return to America, once for two whole years, to recover her broken health. She was a great help in the mission field, having a school for girls, and busying herself in many ways.

In a time of war with England, Americans were not always distinguished from Englishmen, and Dr. Judson, then at Ava, was thrown into prison. It was a wretched building of boards, with no ventilation but through the cracks, and had never been cleaned since it was built. It was to this dreadful place that Mrs. Judson brought the tiny baby Maria for her father's first sight of her. Through all the imprisonment, the loving and courageous wife visited her husband in the midst of all sorts of dangers, as she was the only white woman in Ava. She brought him clean linen as she could, and food, day by day.

One day, having a little more time than usual, she thought she would surprise Dr. Judson by making him a mince pie, as he used to be fond of the dainty at home. She contrived to make it out of buffalo meat and plantains, sending it to him by the one faithful servant. But alas! The poor prisoner was moved to tears at the sight of it and at the thought of his wife's devotion, and could not eat the pie. A fellow-prisoner ate it instead

After a few months, a lion who had been presented to the king was placed in a cage near, and made night and day hideous with his roarings till he died. His cage was so much better than the prison that Mrs. Judson by dint of much begging at last got permission to move her husband into it.

The months wore on, and Dr. Judson was secretly removed to another place to a death-prison. When Mrs. Judson heard it, she set forth, with little Maria in her arms, and partly by boat, partly in a jolting cart, reached the wretched prison. "Why did you come?" her husband cried. "I hoped you would not, for you cannot live here."

The keepers, cruel as they were, yielded at last, and gave her a little room near, which was half full of grain, and there she spent the next six months.

By and by Dr. Judson was sent as an interpreter on a trip, and at last, after many delays and dangers, was released. Coming back to Ava, he hurried to find his wife. He was startled to see a fat half-dressed Burman woman holding a baby too dirty to be recognized as his own child. On the bed lay his wife, worn and pale, her glossy hair gone, her fine head covered with a cotton cap. But she recovered, and the family left the scene of so much misery.

The Judsons began mission work in a new station, and Mrs. Judson was planning a girls' school, and many activities, when Dr. Judson was summoned to Ava on very important business. She urged him to go. While he was absent, she was stricken with fever. With no missionary friend at hand, only the weeping Burmans bewailing "the White Mamma," she passed away. Her husband received the tidings, and hastened home to find the grave under a hopia (hope) tree, surrounded by a rude railing. Little Maria lingered six months, then she was laid beside her mother.

MRS. SARAH HALL BOARDMAN

Reënforcements were not lacking through all the years of Dr. Judson's service. There came out to Calcutta to join the Burman Mission, as soon as might be, Rev. George Dana Boardman, and his wife, who was pronounced by some English friends in Calcutta to be "the most finished and fault-less specimen of an American woman that they had ever known." In 1827 these friends reached Burma. Mr. Boardman died after a few years of very fruitful ministry, and for three years his wife stayed on, making long journeys through drench-ing rains, "through wild mountain passes, over swollen streams, deceitful marshes, craggy rocks, tangled shrubs and jungles." In 1834 she was married to Dr. Judson. She had a very fine knowledge of the Burmese tongue, and could speak and write fluently. She had great power in con-versation, and translated also very accurately. She held meetings with the women for prayer and Bible study. After his eight years of loneliness, Dr. Jud-son found the home ties sweet, and the help he received in his work very great. Mrs. Judson trans-lated part of "Pilgrim's Progress," several tracts, twenty hymns for the Burmese hymn-book, and four volumes of a Scripture Catechism, besides writing cards with short hymns. She learned the language of the Peguans, another tribe, so that she might help them by translating, which she did by superintending the translation of the New Testament and tracts into their strange tongue. Little children came to bless the home, and joy and love reigned there.

But after her twenty years upon the field, Mrs. Judson's health failed. Her husband started home to America with her, but, when reaching the Isle of France, she became so much better that she urged Dr. Judson to return to the work that needed him so much. He expected to do this, but there came a sudden change for the worse. As the vessel neared St. Helena, Mrs. Judson died, and the worn body was laid away in mission ground upon the island, where a stone afterwards marked the spot.

Miss Emily Chubbuck

There is a volume of attractive little sketches which some people used to read before any of you younger readers were born, which bears the name of " Fannie Forester " as the writer. Her real name was Emily Chubbuck. But when she wrote " Alderbrook," and another book of lighter sketches called " Trippings," she used a nom de plume. This young lady was born in Eaton, N. Y., but taught school in Utica in that state, besides writing sketches, poems, and Sunday-school books, so that she was a busy person, as you can see. And a lovely young person she was, too, by all accounts.

When Dr. Judson was at home the last time in America, after his long absence upon the mission field, he travelled about a good deal, and on one of his journeys he read the book called "Trippings," which some one had given him to beguile the way. He thought it a very bright book, and asked his friend about the writer. He said that one who could write as well as that could write better, and he would like to see some of her work on greater themes. His friend told him that he would have the pleasure of meeting "Fannie Forester" before long, as she was a guest in his home at present. When Dr. Judson first saw the attractive and gifted writer, she was undergoing the interesting operation of vaccination. After this was over, he led her to a sofa, saying that he wished to talk with her.

Miss Chubbuck said that she would be delighted to have him do so, and then he spoke about using her talents upon the most worthy subjects. She told him that she had been obliged to write because she was poor and must make a living, and the light and trifling subjects seemed to be most popular. Dr. Judson was full of sympathy for her. He had it in his mind to find some one to write the story of Mrs. Sarah Boardman Judson's life, and offered the opportunity to Miss Chubbuck.

After some time the intercourse thus brought about resulted in marriage, and the cultured and talented, dauntless spirit, schooled in poverty, went back with the missionary, to prove a great help to him in finishing his wonderful work. She soon acquired a good knowledge of the language and prepared Scripture questions for use in the schools.

When her little Emily Frances came, the poet-mother wrote the sweet verses so many have read, called "My Bird."

After Dr. Judson's death and burial at sea, on his way home to regain his health, Mrs. Judson came home, much broken herself, to care for her parents and her children. She died at Hamilton N. Y., in 1854.

XXI

DAVID LIVINGSTONE
Over Thirty Years Missionary in Africa (1840-1874)

PEOPLE who know but one or two missionary names know this one. Anybody might well be ashamed not to know the name, and something about the work, of David Livingstone.

He was a doctor, an explorer and discoverer, a philanthropist who did much for humanity, and, most of all, he was a missionary hero, who gave his life for Africa. What a splendid story is his.

The little David was born of sturdy, earnest Christian parents in the town of Blantyre, Scotland. His father, Neil Livingstone, was a travelling tea merchant in a small way, and his mother was a thrifty housewife. Before he was ten, the boy received a prize for reciting the whole of the one hundred and nineteenth Psalm, "with only five hitches," we are told. He began early to be an explorer, and went all over his native place. He loved to collect flowers and shells. He climbed one day to the highest point in the ruins of

94

Bothwell Castle ever reached by any boy, and carved his name there.

When only ten, he went to work in the cotton mills, and bought a study-book out of his first week's wages. A schoolmaster was provided for evening lessons by the mill-owners. When David could have the master's help, he took it, and when he couldn't, he worked on alone. In this way he mastered his Latin. He was not brighter than other boys, but more determined to learn than many. He used to put a book on the spinning jenny, and catch sentences now and then, as he passed the place in his work. In this way he learned to put his mind on his book no matter what clatter went on around him. When nineteen, he was promoted in the factory. At twenty the young man became an earnest Christian.

It was about this time that Dr. Carey, sometimes called "The Consecrated Cobbler," stirred up the churches on the subject of missions. A good deacon formed a missionary society in Blantyre, and there were missionary talks, and the giving out of missionary books. David Livingstone became so deeply interested that, in the first place, he decided to give to missions all he could earn and save. The reading of the "Life of Henry Martyn" stirred his blood, and then came the appeals of a missionary from China, which thrilled the youth still more. At last he said, "It is my desire to show my attachment to the Cause of Him who died for me by devoting my life to His service." From this time he never wavered in his plan to become a missionary. He got a good preparation, through seven years of study, and became not only a regular minister, but a doctor as well.

The young man wanted to go to China, but the Opium War there prevented. Then Robert Moffat came home and Livingstone heard him plead for Africa and say that he had "sometimes seen in the morning sun the smoke of a thousand villages where no missionary had ever been," and this settled the question for him. He would go to Africa.

His parents consented gladly, but you know that the parting was hard. Look at this picture. It is the evening of November 16, 1840. Livingstone goes home to say good-bye before he leaves his native land for the Dark Continent. He suggests that they sit up all night, and we can see the three talking earnestly together. The father is a man with a missionary's heart in him. At five in the morning they have breakfast, and kneel for family prayers, after David has read Psalms cxxi. and cxxxv. Now the father and son start to walk to Glasgow. Before entering the city, the two say, "Good-bye," and part, never to meet again.

Arrived in Africa, Mr. Livingstone finds some easy work offered at a station, but pushes on seven hundred miles towards Dr. Moffat's station where heathenism is like darkest night. Here the people think him a wizard, able to raise the dead. An old chief says, "I wish you would give me medicine to change my heart. It is proud and angry always." Livingstone shows the way to Jesus. He is the first missionary who ever came into this region. How busy he is as doctor, minister, and reformer. He studies the plants, birds, and beasts. He finds forty-three different kinds of fruit, and thirty-two eatable roots, in one district. He sends specimens to a London college.

This man keeps on exploring, telling of Jesus wherever he goes. When he writes home, his letters are covered with maps of the country. He is learning more about Africa than any one has known before. He studies the African fever, and the deadly tsetse fly, that brings disease. During this time he has the adventure with the lion, often mentioned, the fierce creature rushing on him, biting him and breaking his arm and crushing his shoulder. It cripples him for life, but he says little about it. In putting up a new mission building, he breaks the bone in the same place, but hardly mentions it. Years later, a company of royal surgeons identify the body brought home as that of Livingstone by the scar and the fracture.

For four years this missionary hero toils alone in the beginning of his life in Africa. Then he is happily married to Miss Mary Moffat, daughter of Dr. Moffat who told of the "smoke from the thousand villages, where Jesus was unknown." Now they work earnestly together, in the station called Mabotsa, where the chief Sechele is the first convert. Before he fully learns the "Jesus Way," the chief says to the missionary, "You cannot make these people believe by talking. I can make them do nothing but by thrashing them. If you like, I will call them all together, with my head man, and with our whips of rhinoceros hide we will soon make them all believe." But the missionary teaches him the true way. He goes on exploring new fields, teaching, healing, and helping all the way. He discovers Lake N'gami. He goes into the interior forcing his way through flooded lands, through sharp reeds, with hands raw and bleeding, and with face cut and bloody. He sets himself against the slave-trade, "The open sore of Africa," as he calls it, battling heroically against it and enlisting others in the struggle. His wife and four children must go home, but the man stays, to work on alone. Finally he disappears for three years. He is found in a wonderful way by Henry Stanley, whom he leads to Christ, but he will not return with him to England. He toils on and toils on, weary and worn. One morning in 1874, his African servants find him on his knees in his hut beside his bed. The candle is burning still, but the brave, unselfish life has gone out. They bury their master's heart under a tree, and carry his body on their shoulders a thousand miles to the coast—a nine months' march, then send it home to England. There it sleeps to-day in Westminster Abbey, but the hero and his work live unforgotten and ever-to-be-remembered while the world endures.

XXII

DAVID ZEISBERGER
The Apostle to the Delawares (1745–1805)

WHO is not interested in the Indians? Everybody ought to be, and surely few are not. We like to hear, especially, about the red men of long ago. This little story is

about the man who preached the first Protestant sermon in the state of Ohio, the man who has been called "The Apostle to the Delawares," because he was the first to go to that tribe of Indians.

David Zeisberger was born in Moravia, as long ago as 1721. It is a good thing to know about good men who lived "once upon a time," long years ago. This boy was of a good Protestant family, whose ancestors belonged to the ancient church called The Bohemian Brethren. When David was only five, his parents found that they would be safer in Saxony, so they joined a colony of Moravian emigrants there.

Ten years later, when their son was fifteen, they went to Georgia, joining the American colony there.

But David was left at Herrnhut, Saxony, to be educated. He joined his parents two years after. When he was twenty-four he began his work among the Indians, but it was in troubled times, when anybody might be arrested, if there was the slightest cause to be found. Through some misunderstanding, young Mr. Zeisberger was arrested as a spy in the employ of the French, and was imprisoned in New York for seven weeks.

Governor Clinton released the young missionary, who at once took up his work among the Delawares, and also the Iroquois. Afterwards, the Indians composing the Six Nations made him a " sachem," and a " keeper of their archives " or records of some sort, whatever they were.

The French and Indian War interrupted the missionary labours, but the missionary acted as interpreter, on an important occasion, when Pennsylvania made a treaty with Chief Teedyuseung and his allies. Later Mr. Zeisberger established a mission among the Delawares on the Allegheny River, and still later went to Ohio.

During the War of the Revolution, the Delawares were accused of many things, and the converts were driven from their towns to the British lines. At another time and place, the missionaries were tried as spies and the Christian Indians scattered. Ninety-six came back to gather their corn, but were cruelly put to death. All this was discouraging. The missionary gathered a little remnant and built an Indian town in Michigan. He was a great traveller, you perceive. Mr. Zeisberger came back to Ohio and founded another mission, whose members were obliged to emigrate to Canada after four years. But finally the missionary was allowed to labour for the remaining ten years of his life on the site of a former mission, which he now called Goshen.

This missionary served the Indians for a longer time than any other, even for sixty years altogether. He established thirteen Christian towns, one of them the first Christian settlement in Ohio. He died at eighty-seven, with Christian Indians singing hymns around his bed, " an honour to the Moravian Church and to humanity."

XXIII

ROBERT MORRISON

The Founder of Protestant Missions in China (1807–1834)

WOULD you like to make the acquaintance of a little Scottish lad of long ago? There is good reason for it, you may be sure, for he turned out to be one of our heroes,

brave, persevering, and still unforgotten. This son of Scotch parents was not born in Scotland, but in England, and his people were humble folk, of the name of Morrison, who were glad to welcome their son Robert at his birth, January 11, 1782. That his parents were neither rich nor great made no difference in their son's wishing to do things, nor in his really doing them, but he had to work harder and longer to accomplish them, which did him no harm.

The boy had to begin daily labour early, and was apprenticed to a master who taught him how to make lasts. Robert had no notion, even then, of making this the work of his life; but we believe that he did not shirk his task, though the story goes that he studied while at work. Many have done that, and without slighting their duties. When he was fifteen, Robert's better life began, for then he became a Christian, and united with the Scotch Church. At nineteen he began the study of Latin, Hebrew, and theology, a minister in Newcastle being his teacher. After fourteen months' preparation, he entered what was called a theological academy, to prepare for the ministry. He did not stop with this. His "long, long thoughts" went further, and he decided to become a missionary.

He carried out his purpose and his wish was granted, for in 1804, when he was but twenty-two, he was appointed the first missionary of the London Missionary Society to China. It was this that gave him the claim to be called The Founder of Protestant Missions in China. Don't you think it an honourable title? But although Robert Morrison did a number of "first things," it was not for sake of standing first himself. There were some things that came first, before the young missionary could begin his mission. He went to the missionary college at Gosport, and took two years' training for his work, studying Chinese, among other things. Three years after his appointment the young man sailed for China. But he was not able to go directly there from England. Some difficulties connected with the opium traffic prevented, and he had to go to New York first. It was a long and tiresome journey by this roundabout way. He left London the last day of January, 1807, and it was September before he arrived in Canton.

Here Mr. Morrison assumed the Chinese dress, diet, and habits. He thought it would be economical, and also acceptable to the Chinese, but before long it proved to be neither. It was not good for his health to live on Chinese food altogether, and the Chinese dress was not suitable. It was not pleasing to the Chinese. Of course they knew that he was a foreigner, and it must have seemed like "pretending" for him to dress as they did. Very sensibly, Mr. Morrison returned to his own ways.

About this time the Chinese Government issued an edict forbidding the preaching of the Jesus Religion, and the printing of Christian books. The new missionary therefore wisely set himself about the translation of the Bible, in connection with the continued study of Chinese. His health had suffered from hard study and privations, and besides, it was not safe for him to stay in the empire, and he went to Macao for a year. After this his opportunity came to go back, for he was appointed translator for the East India Company's factory, and this made it safe for him to live in China permanently, with a chance to reach some of the people, and go on with Bible translation.

Mr. Morrison kept this office for twenty-five years, and found time for his Bible-work, also his great Chinese dictionary and other books. His revision of the Book of Acts was the first Scripture portion printed in Chinese by any Protestant missionary. Early in 1814 the whole New Testament was ready. Think what a great work it was

How long do you suppose it was before the first Chinese convert was won? Seven years. He had to have "long patience," you see, but he did not give up. With all his missionary work, Dr. Morrison, as he was made about this time, went on with translating the Bible, a grammar, and other works. Finally the entire Bible was printed, the Old Testament alone making twenty-one volumes. The hardest work of all was the dictionary. It cost fifteen thousand pounds to print it, but Dr. Morrison's part was never reckoned in money. Instead of an alphabet, such as we have, the Chinese make a character stand for a word, and there are over 40,000 characters. A man can get along pretty comfortably with only 10,000, but really ought to know 25,000. There are seven different tones or ways of sounding, and one tone may mean a verb and another a noun. The different tones are sometimes shown by marks. But it is a hard language.

Dr. Morrison took no vacation for seventeen years. Then he went home for two years. He had an audience with George IV, and presented him with a Chinese Bible. He was received with distinction everywhere. Then he went back to the field and died, August 1, 1834, after twenty-five years of heroic service.

XXIV

MRS. HANS EGEDE

Who Shared Her Husband's Labours for Fifteen Years in Greenland (1721–1736)

DID you ever sing " From Greenland's icy mountains " ? Of course you did, for you are not such heathen as never to have sung Bishop Heber's Missionary Hymn. But have you thought very much about those "icy mountains " ?

It is hard to decide whether to speak of the husband or the wife in telling of the missionaries to Greenland in 1721. Think how long ago it was. It was a book that began it. How often it has been a book. It was so with Dr. Judson, and Henry Martyn, and many others.

This book was in the library of a young minister, Hans Egede, in Vaage, on the coast of Norway. It told how a Christian church had been founded in the tenth century in Greenland. Fourteen bishops had ruled over it, but at last the heathen fell upon the Christians, drove them away, and the church was forgotten for centuries. The young minister's heart was stirred with a desire to go and find the lost church. His people called him crazy and even his wife at first refused to think of it. But at last many providences made the wife, as well as the husband, willing and even anxious to go to Greenland, feeling that it was God's will, and their work

Early in 1721 they went, but were almost wrecked in trying to land, and did not land until July. It was far from a "green land" that they found. Not a tree or bush or blade of grass was to be seen, and no remains of the church could be found. The people were greasy savages, smeared with seal oil, dressed in skins, living in queer dwellings more like ant-hills than houses. The wizards tried to kill the missionaries by magic, but failed, of course. Yet it seemed as if hunger and exposure would soon do it, for the ship with supplies was lost. The minister thought they must go back home, but Mrs. Egede said, " Wait a little." She kept up his courage for three weeks and then a ship arrived with stores and colonists, and hope revived.

Mrs. Egede was so anxious that the work should go on that she was willing to have her husband and two boys spend the winter in Greenland huts, that they might learn the language of the natives, and make friends with them. The huts were like great beehives, without any ventilation, heated by seal oil lamps, unimaginably dirty, and shared with dogs and pigs, after two or three families had crowded in. What do you think of the heroism all round ?

After two years the relics of the old church were found, but no one among the living could tell the story of it.

What the missionaries endured can hardly be believed. Once a big, hungry polar bear came into their house, and was gotten out, as by miracle.

One of the younger sons used to draw pictures to help illustrate the father's sermons. Every means possible was used to help the natives. They were very unfriendly for a long time, but in days of distress came and fed the missionaries.

In all times of trial, the brave wife kept up her own courage and helped to make the others courageous. At last helpers came, and the work prospered wonderfully.

Mrs. Egede did not live to see the full dawn of light, dying after fifteen years of faithful service in Greenland.

XXV

DR. JOHN SCUDDER

The First Medical Missionary From America
(1819–1855)

ONCE upon a time, a lady who was ill sent for her physician whose name was Dr. John Scudder. The place was New York City. While in the anteroom for a few minutes, he  took up and read a tract called "The Conversion of the World." It made such a deep impression upon the young doctor's mind that he could not forget it. After thinking it over and thinking it over, he finally decided to give his life to helping in the great Cause, and in 1819 he sailed for Ceylon under the American Board of Foreign Missions. Dr. Scudder was the first medical missionary to go to the foreign field from America. Surely his name should be remembered for this, and also for the fact that in 1820 he was the *only* medical missionary in the world.

After some years Dr. Scudder went from Ceylon to Madras, India. Those who know his name usually associate him especially with India, because that was his last field, and a good part of his thirty-six years of missionary labour was spent there. He made one long stay in the home-land when he had to return, but while in America he did a great deal for the Cause he loved. He loved to talk to children, and while he was at home, spoke to a hundred thousand at different times and places. A lady now living said to me that one of the sweetest memories of her childhood was seeing and hearing dear Dr. Scudder, and having him speak to her when she was a little girl. The good missionary's health failing, he went to Cape of Good Hope, Africa, for medical advice, and was returning to his field when his life ended with a sudden stroke of apoplexy, at Wynburg, South Africa, in 1855.

Dr. Scudder gave more than his own one life to missions. He gave seven sons and two daughters to the work in India, and another record says fifteen grandchildren besides. Isn't it simply splendid to think of such a family as that? At one time a whole mission station was carried on by five sons of the Scudder family, their wives and one sister. Dr. Henry Martyn Scudder was the first son of a missionary to be sent forth as a preacher to the heathen. He was a very skillful physician.

Dr. John Scudder, Jr., was another missionary-physician, and three of his children became missionaries. Rev. William Scudder was another son of this family. He gave twenty-two years of service to India, was then a congregational pastor for eleven years in America. When he was sixty years old he went back to India for nine years of labour, and died in 1895. And one tract was the beginning of all this!

XXVI

JAMES CALVERT
The Printer-Missionary to Fiji (1838–1855)

THERE seems to be no profession or trade that a missionary may not find useful in both home and foreign fields. Now this one, James Calvert, who was born in England a hundred years ago, was apprenticed to a printer, bookbinder, and stationer, for seven years. He had some education first, and seems to have made good use of all his early opportunities.

The young man's heart turned to the foreign mission work, and in good time he was appointed to labour in Fiji, and went bravely to the field to which the Wesleyan Missionary Society sent him. It took three months' travel to reach the island, in 1838. One of the first tasks that came to the heroic missionary was to gather up and bury the bones of eighty victims of a cannibal feast. You see what he had to deal with in his new field, and what the young bride had to face. But they had no thought of turning back—not they

Six months after landing in Fiji, Mr. Calvert had charge of thirteen towns that had no roads at all connecting them, and of twenty-four surrounding islands, some of them a hundred miles away. To reach his island-field, the missionary had only a canoe that was hardly seaworthy, but he used it somehow, and was kept from drowning, and from being killed and eaten by the savages. He and his wife mastered the queer language very soon, and showed very great courage and tact in dealing with the natives.

The name of the king was Thakombau. The conversion of his daughter had a great influence upon the savages. There was a custom in the islands of strangling the women of the household when a king died. Mr. Calvert offered, Fiji fashion, to have one of his own fingers cut off if Thakombau would promise not to strangle any women when the *old* king died. Just this offer showed the cannibals what sort of stuff the man was made of. He did a great deal to abolish the dreadful custom.

When, by and by, the king of the Cannibal Islands became a Christian, he ordered what had been the old "death drums" be used thereafter in calling people together to worship the true God, in whom he now believed. He openly confessed his faith and put away his many wives. Among his last acts was the ceding of Fiji to the Queen of Great Britain.

Mr. Calvert's knowledge of printing and book-binding was very useful indeed, as was the printing-press set up not long after his arrival. The press was carried from one island to another, and thousands and thousands of printed pages were scattered abroad. In 1847 the New Testament, well bound and complete, was ready for the natives.

After seventeen years of labour in Fiji, the missionary spent some time in England, then went on a mission to Africa. In 1855 he attended the Jubilee of Christianity in Fiji. He found over 1,300 churches, ten white missionaries, sixty-five native ones, 1,000 head teachers, 30,000 church-members, and 104,585 church attendants. He died in 1892.

XXVII

FIDELIA FISKE

*The First Unmarried Woman to Go to Persia as a
Missionary (1843–1864)*

"WHAT is she like?" "What is he like?"
These are natural questions to ask
about people, are they not? When we
think about Fidelia Fiske of Persia, and ask what

she was like, we seem to
hear what more than one
friend said of her, that
"she was like Jesus."
She made others think
of what the Saviour was
like when on earth, lov-
ing to pray to His Father,
and "going about doing
good."

The love for missions and the wish to be a missionary came very early to the girl Fidelia, who
heard the work talked about a great deal in the
family from the time she could remember. A rela-
tive who went to the foreign field was often spoken
of, and "a real live missionary" was not a myth to
the child.

The seminary for girls, at Mount Holyoke,
founded by Miss Mary Lyon, was a good training

school for missions. So much was said upon the subject, and the interest of Mary Lyon was so great, that missions seemed to be in the very air. In the first fifteen years there was but one class of graduates that did not have one or more members on the foreign field, while there were hundreds who became Home Mission teachers, or wives of missionaries. It was to this school that Fidelia Fiske went as a pupil, and there her interest grew apace. It was fed, for one thing, by the many letters that came from those who were busy in the work.

One day a missionary from Persia came to the seminary. She wanted a teacher for a girls' school, and begged earnestly for one from Mount Holyoke. Said Fidelia, " If counted worthy, I shall be willing to go." There were all manner of difficulties in the way, but finally she sailed for Persia with Dr. and Mrs. Perkins, and reached Urumia in June, after a journey of about three months, in the year 1843. It was perhaps not a longer trip in those days, but travellers did not go so fast, and it was very tiresome, we may well suppose.

The government of Persia was intolerant, that is, would not bear anything with which it did not agree, and the poor people were very degraded. The parents did not wish their daughters to go to school. Indeed, they thought such a thing very improper indeed.

A few day scholars had been coaxed in before Miss Fiske came, but she was anxious to have a boarding-school. She wrote home to a friend that the first foreign word she learned was daughter, and the next was give. Then she went to the people saying, "Give me your daughters."

It was very hard to get scholars because it was thought such a disgrace for a woman to know how to read, and because it was thought the better way to marry the girls off very early. To be sure, the cruel husbands beat them, and the quarrelsome, coarse women knew nothing better and took it all as a matter of course, but it was all the more pitiful for that.

At last, when the first day set for beginning school was almost over, a Nestorian bishop came bringing two girls saying, "These be your daughters and no man shall take them from you." More came after that—ignorant, dirty, greasy creatures that must be taught to keep clean first of all; but they had souls, and were patiently taught. The people were poor, there were few books, and things were very hard. But the Bible was taught three hours a day, and a great deal of Scripture learned by heart. Miss Fiske and her teachers prayed and toiled on, and by and by a wonderful improvement was seen.

The busy missionary visited the women in the dark, dirty homes, and brought them to her room to pray with and teach them. By and by a Nestorian woman believed the truth and said to others, "The Lord has poured peace into my soul."

One day there was a strange visitor before Miss Fiske's door. It was a Koordish chief, one of the worst of men. He came with gun and dagger, and acted as if he would defy everybody. But he brought his daughter and left her in the school. His heart was reached at last, and he was wonderfully changed. He kept saying, "My great sins— my great Saviour," and he led the rest of his family to the Lord Jesus. One time this man was praying in a meeting. When he rose from his knees he said, "O God, forgive me. I forgot to pray for Miss Fiske's school." He knelt again, and prayed earnestly for it.

In the year 1846 a most wonderful blessing came to the school. The Holy Spirit touched the girls' hearts. They looked for places to pray, and used the teachers' rooms for prayer-closets, and even the wood-cellar. It was not the only time that many conversions occurred. When the school was nineteen years old twelve such seasons as this had come, and more than two-thirds of the scholars had learned to know Jesus Christ. Miss Fiske was full of joy, but she was much worn out. One time, after several services, she was so tired that it seemed as if she could not sit up through the preaching service. A woman came and sat down behind her, so that she could lean on her, and said, "If you love me, lean hard."

Worn out, Miss Fiske returned home, and failing to recover strength she died in 1864, in Shelburne, Mass., where she was born. She was in her forty-eighth year. A grieving Nestorian girl wrote to America: "Is there another Miss Fiske in your country?"

XXVIII

DR. MARCUS WHITMAN
Who Saved Oregon for His Country (1836–1847)

WHAT is an explorer? One who travels over a country to discover what is in it? You will say so, if you go to the dictionary man, who is a good one to consult in very many cases.  Think up some explorers that you have heard of. Perhaps you will begin with Columbus, who was certainly a famous one. But if the discovery of this land in the first place had not been followed afterwards, through many years, by other explorations and explorers, we might none of us be living just where we are now.

Among the explorers of the early part of the nineteenth century were two men named Lewis and Clark. Their names are always coupled together, for they went together, and they made their way far West, in 1802–4. Of course they found Indians in great numbers. The Indians had begun by this time to know more of the white men because of the many explorers who passed their way. From some of these the red men got some knowledge of God and the Bible. Lewis and Clark told them that in God and the Bible, lay the secret of the white man's power. This was one of the most important things that these two explorers did. It made the red men long to know more of God and His Book. Every Sunday the Hudson Bay Company put up a flag to show what day it was, and the Indians called it " Flag Day " when they saw it float. There was a trapper who spent a great deal of time reading the mysterious Book and talking to the Unseen Being. The Indians wanted to know more about this new religion and were told that by and by missionaries would come to teach them. So they waited. Around their council fires they talked and wondered about the coming messengers. And they waited. But it was in vain, and years and years went by.

In 1832 the red men decided to send five Nez Perces far East to find the white man's Book, and beg for teachers. So they went, but only four reached St. Louis. They found General Clark there, and their old friend, superintendent now of Indian affairs, treated them kindly. But when they told him for what they had taken the long journey, he did not make the errand public. Why he did not, we cannot imagine. He entertained them, as others seem to have done also, and took them to see the sights. They were taken to the cathedral and shown the pictures of the saints, but the story of the Saviour was not told, nor was the white man's Book given them. Two of the four died, and the remaining two sadly prepared to return to their camp-fires. As they were leaving the office of General Clark, one of them spoke such touching words of farewell that a young man who heard them took them down, and here they are:

"I came to you over a trail of many moons from the setting sun. You were the friend of my fathers who have all gone the long way. I came with one eye partly opened for more light for my people who sit in darkness. I go back with both eyes closed. How can I go back to my blind people? . . . The two fathers who came with us —we leave asleep beside your great water and wigwam. They were tired in many moons and their moccasins wore out. My people sent me to get the white man's Book of Heaven. . . . You showed me images of good spirits, and pictures of the good land beyond, but the Book was not among them to tell us the way. I am going back the long sad trail to my people. . . . You make my feet heavy with gifts, but the Book is not among them. When I tell my poor people . . . that I did not bring the Book, no word will be spoken. . . . One by one they will rise up and go out in silence. My people will die in darkness, and they will go on the long path to the hunting grounds. No white man will go with them, and no white man's Book will show the way. I have no more words."

The young man who copied the words sent them East, and when asked about it. General Clark said that they were true. The story roused the Christian people. It was not strange, was it? Several people promised to go, five at least, but only two went to answer this call. In a log cabin, in New York State, where now is the town called Rushville, over thirty years before, was born the boy who was now to be a Pathfinder to the great West. The country was wild and new. The father was a tanner and currier, or leather-dresser. It was lonesome in the house, and the mother used to go and sit binding shoes in her husband's little shop. One evening when she came back, having left the baby Marcus in his quaint little cradle, she was frightened to see that a log had tumbled out of the big open fireplace, and had set fire to the lower end of the wooden cradle. The baby was almost choked with the smoke, but his life was saved for a great mission.

At seventeen the boy became a Christian. His heart was set on becoming a minister, but his brothers, fearing he would have to be a "charity student," discouraged him. The way opened for the study of medicine, and he took his diploma, really practicing eight years or more. At one time he was associated with his brother in running a sawmill—not knowing that this experience, too, would be a help to him by and by. Hindered in his wish to study for the ministry, his heart turned towards missionary work. He offered to go anywhere the American Board would send him. He fairly panted for such service, and his passion for adventure and exploration only increased his zeal.

The opportunity had now come, and Dr. Whitman started from St. Louis, April 8, 1835. But this
was just a little preparatory trip to see what could
be done. He returned after a journey of 3,000
miles, and spent a busy winter in preparation. He
secured the company of Rev. H. H. Spalding and
wife, and Mr. William Gray, and the best compan-
ionship of all, in the bride who consented with all
her heart to go with him.

Try to imagine that journey. Think what supplies the company must take, and the untrodden,
lonesome way before them. Part of the way the
ladies rode in one of the two wagons, but much of
the trip was made on horseback. At night came
the encampment beside a fire, where buffalo meat,
their chief subsistence, was cooked. Dr. Whitman
proved to be an excellent cook. His wife said he
cooked every piece of meat a different way. The
waterproof blanket spread on the ground, with
another blanket above, served for a bed for each
traveller. In crossing rivers, the women rode the
tallest horses to keep from getting wet. After four
months and three thousand miles of travel, stopping
at Fort Walla Walla, crowds of Indians met them,
and some asked, "Have you brought the Book of
God?" At last the journey ends in Oregon, the
rude shelter is put up for housekeeping, the missionary work is begun. Little Alice Clarissa is
born, but after a few years is drowned in the river.
After a while seven orphan children are adopted,
and at one time there are eleven of these in the
family. At one time the only meat to be had i

horse-flesh, which they learn to eat, because there is nothing else. But not once do one of the missionaries regret coming.

Now comes Dr. Whitman's great, patriotic, daring service. He learns that it is the intention to secure Oregon to Great Britain. His famous ride in the dead of winter, 1843, on horseback across the continent, follows. After incredible hardships, he reaches Washington, with ears, nose, fingers and feet frozen. But he sees Daniel Webster, Secretary of State, and President Tyler, and secures the promise not to cede Oregon to England. He promises to take a wagon train of emigrants across the desert, and takes it, a thousand strong, proving that it is not impossible, as has been thought. Oregon is saved to the United States.

Now follow years of mission work, of labours abundant and of every kind. But difficulties begin to thicken. Trouble with the Indians breaks out. There are reasons and incidents too numerous to tell. But the sad end is the death of Dr. Whitman and his wife, with others, who died by red men's hands, in 1847.

Remember this hero-patriot and pathfinder of that great country " where rolls the Oregon."

XXIX

ELIZA AGNEW

Called " The Mother of a Thousand Daughters" in Ceylon (1850–1883)

WOULD you like to hear what the study of geography did for a little girl, who was born as long ago as the year 1807? It was in New York City that this girl studied her

geography lessons, and learned about the great world. Perhaps she was the only one in the class that thought about the great number of heathen people in the countries far away that were so interesting in many ways, but Eliza Agnew thought about them. She thought about them so much and so earnestly, that at last she made up her mind to go as a missionary as soon as she was old enough. She was eight when she made this resolve.

The study of geography, as far as the book was concerned, was finished long before Eliza was old enough to carry out her purpose, but she never forgot it or gave it up. By and by the way opened, and Miss Agnew sailed away to the Island of Ceylon, where, as you know, there are pearl fisheries

But this missionary was a seeker after pearls of a
different sort, and she found them, too.   The pearls
were the souls of girls in that tropical island, who
were led to Jesus Christ by this missionary.

For all of forty-one years Miss Agnew was the
principal of a girls' boarding-school in Oodooville,
on the island, and, altogether, she taught a thousand
girls.   In some cases she had the children, and in
others the grandchildren, of her first pupils.   She
was so gentle, and loving, and good, that they all
called her "Mother."   This meant that they felt
themselves to be her daughters, and this is the
reason that the good missionary was called at last
"The Mother of a Thousand Daughters."

She was very, very happy in her work of "finding pearls," and it was said that no girl who took
the full course in the school went out without becoming a Christian.   During the forty-one years,
six hundred girls came out on the Lord's side, and
were received into the church as members.   Many
of these girls became teachers in village schools,
and in other places.   Many became the wives of
native teachers, preachers, catechists, doctors, law-
yers, merchants and farmers, who brought up their
children "in the fear of the Lord, faithfully."   Some
were even taken as wives by the chief men of the
district, and had great opportunities to do good.
In northern Ceylon forty Bible readers gave their
time to this work.   In forty-three years Miss Agnew
never went home at all.   She died in 1883, aged
seventy-six.   Her watchword was: "I'll tell the
Master."

XXX

JAMES HANNINGTON
"The Lion-hearted Bishop" of Africa (1882-1885)

THE boy who was afterwards "The Lion-hearted Bishop," was known among his mates as "Mad Jim." This was because he was so very fond of fun and adventure, and was never afraid of any risk that promised to bring what he set his heart upon. He was a great lover of nature and would climb daringly to get a good view, or scramble recklessly to get a fine specimen. This merry boy was born in England in 1847. When he was fifteen he left school, because he was not fond of study, and was put in his father's counting room at Brighton. He had the spirit of dauntless perseverance in anything that interested him, and would do anything rather than be foiled in what he set out to accomplish. When quite a young man, he was at one time commander of a steam yacht, and at another, captain of a battery. In these positions he showed that he had a gift in managing men, and of making the best of difficult circumstances. But he did not like business any better than he liked study. From boyhood there was one sheet-anchor that held this merry and irrepressible boy, and that was his devoted love for his mother. That speaks well for him, does it not?

Outwardly, this boy and youth never neglected religious duties, but he was not at peace. He felt that he was living apart from God. When he was twenty-one, he made the important decision of his life, and began to prepare for the ministry of the Church of England. At Oxford he gained great influence over his fellow students. You can see that he was a born leader.

In 1874 Mr. Hannington took a small parish in Devonshire. In his case, as in that of Dr. Scudder, what seemed a small thing led to very great ones, and changed the course of the life. This gentleman, a year after he began to serve his small parish, had a talk with two ladies about missions. It led him to study the whole subject carefully—something he had not done before. Three years later his whole soul was moved by the story of the cruel death of two missionaries in Africa. He thought to himself, "I believe that I have some characteristics and some experience that would fit me to go as a missionary to those wilds." But his wife could not go with him. What should be done? The two talked it over. The wife bravely gave her consent to an absence of five years, and the husband as courageously decided to go to Africa. He was sent out as leader of a party of six to reënforce the Central African Mission at Bubaga. An appeal in the London *Times* brought in subscriptions that allowed the purchase of a boat for lake travel. In 1882 the party sailed for Zanzibar.

But on arriving, Mr. Hannington was taken ill. His strength was wasted by African fever and other disorders, and he had to return home next year. He recovered his health, happily, and went back to the Dark Continent, this time as the Bishop of Equatorial Africa. Freretown was the place where he decided to make his home, and the indefatigable missionary began to make a visitation of all the mission stations within 250 miles of the seacoast.

There was one important station on a mountain, 2,500 feet above the plain, which was very hard to reach. The Lion-hearted Bishop had to travel over dreadful swamps, and over 200 miles of desert full of dangers, to reach the place. But, nothing daunted, he took the journey and made the visit.

The missionary had a variety of experiences, and one that you will think very odd. He wished a Christmas pudding and determined to make it himself, since there was no one else to do it. There was nothing to make it of but sour raisins and spoiled flour, but he made the pudding. I could not find out who ate it. Perhaps the natives did not " mind."

And now the missionary was strongly possessed with the idea of opening a shorter route to Uganda, through a higher and healthier region

than that which cost him his health when travelling it before. With 200 porters he started from
Mombassa. After many adventures the party
reached Victoria Nyanza, and Bishop Hannington,
with a portion of his men, pushed on towards
Uganda. Nothing was heard of them for some
time, when, November 8, 1885, four men, out of
the fifty who went with the Bishop, returned
with the heart-breaking news of his death, and
that of their fellows.

It seems that the natives had become angry over
the coming of so many foreigners to their country.
They decided to put a stop to it, and the cry was
"Kill the missionaries." It was believed that
they were the forerunners of the invaders who
were to be driven out and kept out. Especially in
Uganda did this feeling run high. It was just at
the most critical time that Bishop Hannington's
arrival was announced, and it was decided that he
must die. The chief was unwilling at first, and
proposed sending him back. But there was the
booty, and the temptation to take it proved too
much. The brave Bishop was enticed away from
his men, kept in a filthy hut for eight days, then
killed with his own rifle. His men were also put
to death. He died fearlessly, telling the soldiers to
tell the chief he "died for the Baganda, and pur-
chased a road to Uganda with his life." The
Baganda were the men of the place.

XXXI

JOSEPH HARDY NEESIMA

Founder of " The One Endeavour Company " of Japan
(1874–1890)

HOW do you suppose it would feel to be born in Japan? You cannot imagine anything so strange. But perhaps you can imagine a little of a Japanese boy's feelings after hearing what he thought about, as a little fellow, in that far-away island kingdom.

When this boy, whom we know as Joseph Hardy Neesima, was little, he used to think a great deal about religion, but it was not the true religion, for he did not know anything about it. His parents taught him from babyhood to pray to the idol-gods made by hands, and to worship the spirits of his ancestors—his grandfathers and grandmothers ever so far back. He often went with them to the graveyards to pray to these spirits. Sometimes the small boy would rise very early, and go to a temple three and a half miles away, and pray to the idols, coming back in time for breakfast. Of course it did him no good, but he did the best he

knew, and kept on bravely, without minding how
hard it was. Yet some boys and girls in this
country have been known to think that it was too
hard to get up early enough on Sabbath morning to
be in good time for Sabbath school at half-past nine.

Neesima was ten years old when Commodore
Perry, of the United States, came sailing into the
Bay of Yedo, with a message to the emperor from
our President; and the closed doors of Japan, that
had long been shut against foreigners, were first
pushed open—to open wider by and by. Neesima
was much stirred up over the coming of the commodore. He wished above everything to become
a brave soldier and fight for his country. The
Japanese seem to be born with love of country in
their hearts—most of them. The ten-year-old boy
went often to the temple of the god of war, and
asked him to make him a good soldier, ready to
fight. But one day he read the saying of a Chinese
writer, who showed that one could become a braver
man by studying books, which would help him to
conquer thousands, than by practicing with a sword
which could only kill one man at a time. Neesima
decided that he would stop sword-practice and
study books. So he did, and with all his might.
Sometimes he did not go to bed till after cock-
crowing in the morning—a foolish thing, but it
shows how much in earnest he was! He began to
study the Dutch language, and sometimes ran away
from the office where he was, to take his lesson
from the Dutch master, after which he was beaten
more than once, by order of the prince.

Time went on and Neesima was fifteen. About this date, he borrowed some Chinese books to read. He opened one of them and read the first sentence. It was " In the beginning God created the heaven and the earth." The boy had often asked his parents who made him, and who made all things. They could not satisfy him with their answers. This sentence seemed an answer. He said to himself " God made all things. God made me ; I must be thankful to Him, and obey Him. I must pray to Him." As he said afterwards, from this time " his mind was fulfilled to read English Bible " and " burned to find some missionary or teacher to make him understand." But he waited and watched six years, in darkness, not finding any one to tell him about the Christian's God, although praying all the time to this unknown Being. Do you not think that he did the best he could ?

When he was twenty-one, Neesima asked leave to go to Hakodate, but was refused, and flogged besides, for the mere asking. But at last he got away safely, telling his mother he would be gone a year. It was ten years before he came back. While in Hakodate, he made up his mind to go to America to find the Christian's God. If a Japanese was found trying to leave his country he was put to death, in those days ; but a friend rowed Neesima out to a ship at midnight and he got on board. There the captain hid him, so that the officers who came next morning to look for him did not discover him. Arrived in Shanghai, the young man took passage for Boston. The ship was owned by

a merchant prince named Honourable Alpheus
Hardy. God guided the youth to him, to find out
about God. Mr. Hardy took him into his own home
and for ten years gave him the best education to
be had anywhere.

After some years, Neesima took his stand for
Christ by uniting with the Church. After he was
graduated from Amherst College, he entered Andover Theological Seminary. Two years before
graduation, he was sent for by the Japanese
Embassy that came to Washington. He did not
fall on his face before them, as a Japanese would,
but greeted them as an American and a Christian
should. They asked him to go with them to the
capitals of Europe, and a year of wonderful travel
followed. But Neesima steadily refused to journey
on Sunday. He always stopped off and followed
on Monday.

After being graduated from the theological seminary, Neesima was made a member of the Japan
Mission of the American Board, and Mr. Hardy
undertook his support. His great desire now was
to found a Christian college in Japan. The first
speech he ever made before the Board put him all
in a tremble, so that he could not do anything but
pray by way of preparation. But when the time
came, he had such a feeling for the poor people of
his country that he said of himself, " I shed much
tears instead of speaking for them, and before I
closed my poor speech (less than fifteen minutes
long) about $5,000 were subscribed on the spot."

When Neesima went back to Japan in 1874 he

found great changes everywhere: a new calendar, the Sabbath made a holiday, newspapers being printed, an army and navy created, a mint established, lighthouses, railways, telegraphs, and other new things in operation in the country. The young graduate was offered a high position by the government, but kept steadfastly to his purpose, and founded the Christian college which was called The Doshisha, meaning "One Endeavour Company." Was not that a good, active name? It was founded in Kyoto, with eight students in the beginning. Of the first 178 who were graduated in seventeen years, all but about ten were Christians. In twenty-five years, 4,611 students entered, and of the 936 graduates, 147 engaged in teaching, and ninety-five preached the Gospel.

For the first six years the work was hard, but Neesima never wavered. Prosperity came at last, and large gifts for the institution. Finally the founder's health gave way. The doctor said he might live several years if he would rest for two years, but the brave man decided to do what he could while life lasted, and kept on, in weakness and pain, labouring for his beloved college. He died, January 23, 1890, with the words " Peace, joy, heaven " on his lips. Three thousand people followed his body to its resting-place. "The workman dies but the work goes on."

XXXII

MELINDA RANKIN

The First Protestant Missionary to Mexico (1812–1888)

HAVE you ever heard the date "1812" mentioned as an important one in history? There was war in our country then, and when you study history, you find some generals mentioned who became famous. But in that year a baby was born among the hills of New England, who helped to bring peace to many, even in the midst of wars and troubles. It was Melinda Rankin, who found her life-work in the sunny land of the Aztecs in old Mexico, the land of adobe huts and degraded people.

She said of herself, in later years of life, that when she gave her heart to the Lord Jesus she was filled with a desire to tell others about Him where His name was not known. She could not settle down in comfort and quietness in her New England home. But it was not till she was twenty-eight that her first chance came. Then there came a call for missionary teachers to go to the Mississippi Valley. Miss Rankin responded, and went first to Kentucky and then on to Mississippi.

When the war between our country and Mexico was over, the soldiers coming home told much of the Mexican people, how ignorant and priest-ridden they were. Hearing these things, Miss Rankin was much stirred up. She wrote articles for the papers, and tried to rouse an interest among churches and missionary societies. She did not succeed very well. No one seemed ready to go to the needy field. At last she exclaimed, " God helping me, I will go myself."

But Mexico was in a lawless state. It was positively dangerous for Protestants to go there, for they were forbidden by the government to bring Christianity in any form whatever. As Miss Rankin could not get into Mexico, she decided to get as near to it as she could. She went to Texas, and settled down at Brownsville, on the Rio Grande River, just opposite Matamoras, Mexico.

Not a hotel was to be found, and it was hard to find shelter of any sort. Miss Rankin never once thought of giving up. The boys would say that she was " a plucky sort." Finally she found two rooms which she was allowed to rent. She took one for a bedroom and the other for a schoolroom. But she had no furnishings whatever. She was taken care of and her wants supplied, though not luxuriously. She wrote, " A Mexican woman brought me a cot, an American sent me a pillow, and a German woman said she would cook my meals ; and so I went to my humble cot with feelings of profound gratitude."

There were many Mexicans in the city of Brownsville, and when a school was opened, the day after Miss Rankin found rooms, the Mexican girls came to her in numbers that really surprised her. It was very encouraging.

One day a Mexican mother came to her, bringing " her saint " as she called it.

" I have prayed to this all my life," she said, " and it has never done me any good. May I change it for a Bible ? "

Miss Rankin was so pleased that she gave her two Bibles, because the woman said, " I have a friend over in Matamoras that wants a Book too." This was the first Bible that the missionary got across the border, but it was not the last. This little beginning made her think deeply about going on. If only she could get God's Word across the river into the country, it would be the best possible thing. There was a law against it, but Miss Rankin thought that no power on earth had a right to keep out the Bible. She decided to give herself to the work of getting it across the river.

" You'd better send bullets and gunpowder to Mexico instead of Bibles," said a man on this side, who had little faith. But the missionary did not think so, and did not take his advice. Somehow she found means to send over hundreds of Bibles, and hundreds of thousands of pages of tracts, which the American Bible Society, and Tract Society, furnished to the intrepid distributor. For you may know that it took dauntless courage to do it.

Mexicans came over to the missionary's door, asking for God's Book. Orders for books, with money in payment, came from Monterey, and other towns. A Protestant portrait painter helped on the work by carrying over with him great quantities.

Not being able to get a Christian colporteur speaking Spanish, she herself went out as agent for the American and Foreign Christian Union, with great success. Her school was left with her sister. But troubles came. The sister died. Miss Rankin was stricken with yellow fever, and was near death. Mexican women nursed her lovingly, and she recovered. But the Civil War in our land came on, and the missionary was driven out of Texas. She went across the river, and her work on Mexican soil began.

In Monterey, with 40,000 people, she founded the First Protestant Mission, under difficulties and dangers uncounted. She was driven from house to house, but came back home and collected money for buildings for the Mission. Converts multiplied, and went themselves from house to house, and from ranch to ranch, teaching others. The work spread. Some Bible readers wrote, " We can hardly get time to eat or sleep, so anxious are the people for God's Word."

In 1871, through disturbances and battles, she was kept safe, but next year returned home, where, after telling her story often, she passed away, in 1888, aged seventy-six. It was she who said, " The word discouragement is not in the dictionary of the kingdom of heaven." A church of one hundred and seventy Mexican members was handed over to the Presbyterian Board of Missions when she left Mexico.

XXXIII

ALEXANDER MACKAY

" The Engineer-Missionary" to Africa (1876–1890)

WE like to go back to beginnings, and see how things started. Most of all, it is interesting to know how people began, as children. You will be astonished to hear some things about the childhood of the man called " The Engineer-Missionary," and will be interested as well. He was a minister's boy, born in Scotland, in Aberdeenshire, in 1849, and when he was three years old he read the New Testament! When he was only seven, he read Milton's great poem, " Paradise Lost," and the historian Gibbon's book about the Roman Empire, also Robertson's " History of the Discovery of America." It is not so surprising, is it, that the Scotch boy should find this last book fascinating? But think of reading the others, when, in our Sunday-schools, he would only be in the primary department! Very early indeed, his minister-father taught him geography, astronomy and geometry, but in a very attractive way, and often out-of-doors, which, you will think, was not so bad. Sometimes the father would stop to trace out the path of the heavenly bodies in the sky by lines in the sand, or the course of a newly-discovered river in far-off Africa, using his cane to trace it.

Well, this bright boy grew up, as other boys do, and as he grew older he listened with a great deal of interest to the talks of wise men who visited his father at the manse, and to their letters when they were received. These talks and letters were about wonderful things in nature, and one of the men who knew a great deal about these wonders was Hugh Miller. You may hear about him after you get farther on in your studies, if you do not know his name now.

When the time came to choose a profession, young Alexander Mackay decided upon engineering. You may be sure, too, that he became a good engineer. He did thoroughly what he undertook. For some time he had an important position on the continent, in Berlin. But in 1875 he heard a call to Africa. It was found that the natives of that country, especially near Lake Victoria Nyanza, needed to be taught, not only Christianity, but various industries, so that they could work with their hands. Africans were not accustomed to doing very much work, especially the men—the women worked with their hands very busily. A call was sent to the Christians at home to send out a man to teach the natives of Mombassa how to work with their hands and how to do business. Mr. Mackay offered himself, but another was sent first. Soon after, he was offered a position with a large salary, but would not take it. He said that he wished to be ready when his chance came to go to Africa.

The next year, 1876, he was sent out, the youngest man in the company of pioneers, but on the march, after leaving Zanzibar, he was taken very ill and was sent back to the coast, where he recovered. He was told not to return before the rainy season was over, because the roads were so bad. No roads can well be worse than African roads, that are often mere tracks that zigzag around the trees and stumps, for no native would think of taking anything out of the way. He goes round instead. But Mr. Mackay built 230 miles of road, and in November he reached Uganda. Here he was on the track of Mr. Henry M. Stanley, the man who found Livingstone, you remember. Mr. Stanley was the first man from abroad to visit Uganda, and he sent back word to England that Mtesa, the king, wanted missionaries sent there. Mr. Mackay said that wherever Mr. Stanley had been, he found it easier to go, because the natives had been so kindly treated by the first visitor. The Engineer-Missionary had studied the language before coming and was able to print parts of the Bible, cutting the type himself. He read and explained the Scriptures to King Mtesa, who showed much interest in the truth.

But you must know that to the natives the newcomer's greatest achievement, in the earlier time, was building a wagon, painted red and blue, and drawn by oxen. They thought this was perfectly wonderful.

After six years the king died and his son, who took his place, was very weak and vacillating, so that no one could depend upon him. He threatened to send Mr. Mackay out of his country, but the missionary held his ground. His engineering work was so valuable that the king often took advantage of it, in spite of his threats.

In two years the persecutions broke out afresh, and finally, in 1887, the Arabs persuaded Mwanga to expel Mr. Mackay. He locked the Mission premises and went to the southern end of the lake. Here he stayed for three years. He was busy translating and printing the word of God, teaching the Christian refugees from Uganda, and also the natives of the place, meanwhile working at house-building, brick-making, and in the building of a steam launch. In February, 1890, an attack of malarial fever caused the death of the brave, gentle missionary, called by Mr. Stanley "the greatest since Livingstone."

XXXIV

TITUS COAN
(*Of Hawaii*)

*Pastor of the Largest Church in the World in the
Middle of the Nineteenth Century (1835–1882)*

WHEN you read the heading of this chapter, you will certainly want to keep on till you know how many members there were in the "largest church" in the middle of the nineteenth century. But first of all, you must know something about the man who was the pastor of it, and so we will begin at the beginning.

In 1801 in Killingworth, Connecticut, was born the boy who afterwards had the distinction just mentioned. But you may be sure that it was not "distinction" that he cared for, by the time it came to him. As this Connecticut boy grew up and became a minister, he heard the call in his heart to go far off to those who did not know what he knew of the true God and the Saviour Jesus Christ. His first mission was to one of the darkest parts of the earth—Patagonia. You know where that is, at the tip end of the Continent of South America. It was truly a dreadful place, where the ferocious savages wandered about, as wild and wicked as you can imagine, and worse.

For several months Mr. Coan and his associate Mr. Arms, lived among these fierce natives of the eastern coast. But the natives would not believe that they came to do them good, and so great was the danger of death at their cruel hands that the two missionaries were obliged to leave, and they finally escaped in 1834. They returned to New London, Connecticut.

Mr. Coan's desire and determination to be a missionary was not lessened by this experience. It was rather strengthened by the sight of what men were without Christianity. There came another call, and the way opened in another direction—that of the Hawaiian Islands. A year and a month after the return from Patagonia, on June 6, 1835, Mr. and Mrs. Coan landed in Honolulu, and the next month went to Hilo, the station where they were to work.

Some missionaries had been there before, for a little time. Some schools has been established, and about a fourth of the people could read. There was a church of thirty-six members. All this meant a good beginning, but not a big beginning, and there remained much to be done. In three months, Mr. Coan began to speak the native language. He must have been a bright man, and a very diligent one as well, to get on so fast with the strange tongue of those islanders. He spent as much time as he possibly could among them, and tried to see and become acquainted with as many as possible. Before the year was over, this missionary had been all round the island, by canoe and on foot. It was a trip of three hundred miles. In this parish was the largest active volcano-crater in the world.

This missionary was one of the busiest you ever heard of. In eight days he preached forty-three times. In a trip of thirty days he examined twenty schools, and over twelve hundred scholars, talked personally with multitudes of people, and ministered to many sick.

So he went on, preaching, teaching, praying, his wife helping in many ways. In the latter part of the year 1835, Mr. Coan made a tour of his field, and felt that a great blessing was coming. Multitudes gathered to hear his message. One morning he had to preach three times before breakfast, which he took at ten o'clock.

It was in 1837 that the great revival really came. It continued in wonderful power for two years. It has been said that this missionary held a camp-meeting lasting two years. Almost the whole population of Hilo and Puna crowded to hear the Word of God. Of course there was no church building large enough to hold them all. The sick and the disabled were brought to the meetings on the backs of kind neighbours and friends, or were borne upon litters (like that man in the Bible who was " borne of four "). At any time of day or night, if a bell were rung, thousands of people would gather to hear preaching. Was it not wonderful ?

In two years, seven or eight thousand natives had professed to be Christians, but thus far only a few had been taken into the church. The missionary wished to be very sure that the people were true followers of Jesus. So the very greatest care was used in choosing the ones to be received, and in examining them, watching and teaching them. On the first day of July, 1838, 1,705 persons united with the church, and that afternoon 2,400 communicants sat down at the Lord's table together.

In five years 7,557 were received, and now you know the membership of the largest church in the world in the middle of the nineteenth century. And nearly all proved faithful. Seven churches were made out of this one, six of them with native pastors. The good missionary died at Hilo in 1882.

XXXV

JOHN G. PATON
" The Saint John of the New Hebrides " (185?–1907)

LET us look at some fascinating pictures which this wonderful missionary has left for us in the story of his life. The first one is that of his little home in dear old Scotland,  in the county of Dumfries. We see the boy's birthplace, a little cottage in the parish of Kirkmahoe, where, on May 24, 1824, he saw the light. This place is in the background. In the foreground stands the home in the busy village of Torthorwald, whither the child was taken when five years old, and where the staunch, godly Scotch parents, in the forty years that went by, brought up their five sons and six daughters, and saw them go out into the world.

The cottage has stout oaken ribs, which the years of peat smoke have " japanned " until they shine, and they are too hard to drive a nail into them. The roof is thatched, the walls are of stone, plastered, or pointed, with sand, clay and lime

There in the front of the three roomed house we
see the mother's domain, kitchen, parlour and bedroom in one, and in the rear room, the father's
stocking-frames, five or six of them, which busy
fingers keep in use betimes.   The merchants of the
county know and prize the good work of those
frames.

There is a middle room, called a closet, which
is "the sanctuary"; for here, in the bare little
place, with only space for bed, table, and chair,
with a small window to light it, the father goes by
himself and "shuts to the door" daily, and often
three times a day.   The children know that he is
praying, and sometimes hear his voice through the
shut door, but it is too sacred a thing to talk about.
The one who is to become a great missionary never
loses the memory of that place and those prayers,
and often says to himself, "He walked with God,
why may not I?"

The thatched cottage with oaken ribs is the
scene of busy days and happy Sabbaths, when
churchgoing, and Bible stories and the Shorter
Catechism at home, are not tasks but pleasures.
Then we see the school days, and, when the boy is
twelve, the learning of the father's trade, with long
hours daily, and all the spare minutes spent in
study of first lessons in Greek and Latin.   The boy
has early decided to become a missionary, and even
at the stocking-frames learns some things in the
use of tools, and the watching of machinery, worth
much to him in coming days and far-off fields.

The second picture that we look upon, as we fol-

low the early days of the youth who is to be a mis
sionary to distant savages, shows us many things.
We see him working, saving, studying, going to
school, earning money, going through all sorts of
struggles and trials, teaching school, managing the
unruly scholars without beating them with the
heavy stick given him with which to "keep order,"
and finally, we behold him as a city missionary.
His district is dreadfully poor and degraded, and
after a year's work, there are but six or seven won
to churchgoing to show for it.

But the indefatigable young city missionary
struggles on. A kind Irishwoman whose husband
beats her, when drunken, and whose life is a toil-
some one, gives the lower floor of her house for
meetings. Classes are organized, meetings held in
various places, visits are made continually, and the
work grows wonderfully. The churches near receive many new members from this field, and eight
lads work their way through educational courses to
enter the ministry. So ten busy, burdened, and
useful, happy years pass by.

Now comes a third picture, which shows us the
call to the foreign field. The Reformed Church of
Scotland, in which Mr. Paton has been brought up,
calls for a new missionary to help Mr. Inglis in the
New Hebrides. Not one can be found, after most
earnest prayer and the use of all possible means.

Young Mr. Paton is deeply interested. He
hears the heavenly Father's voice saying, " Since
none better can be got, rise and offer yourself." He
almost answers aloud, " Here am I, send me," but

is afraid of being mistaken. At last, however, he feels impelled to make the offer, and he is joyfully received and accepted. His city mission parishioners rebel, and every effort is made to keep him from leaving them, but nothing now can dissuade him. His parents bid him Godspeed, saying, "We long ago gave you away to the Lord, and in this matter also, would leave you to God's disposal." Then he hears for the first time that at his birth he was dedicated to missionary work, if God should call, and that they have prayed ever since, that their first-born might be prepared and sent as a messenger to the heathen. The young missionary's happy marriage follows, and his departure with his bride for the cannibal island of Tanna, New Hebrides, in the far South Seas. He is now thirty-two and the time is December, 1857.

Let us turn to the fourth picture, which shows us the island of Tanna. Dr. Inglis, and some native Christian teachers from the partly Christianized island of Aneityum, go with Mr. Paton, while Mrs. Paton stays for a while with the missionaries' wives who can tell her much of mission work, and she joins her husband later. The first view of the naked, painted, miserable savages gives a feeling of horror as well as of pity. They come crowding round to see the building of a wooden, lime-plastered house, chattering like monkeys.

Whatever interchange there is, must be by signs at first. One day the clever missionary notices a man lifting up some article that is strange, and asking another " Nungsi nari enu ? " He decides that this means " What is it ? " and tries it again and again upon different natives. They always answer by giving the name he wishes. Again he hears a stranger asking, " Se nangin ? " pointing to the missionary. " He is asking my name," thinks Mr. Paton. It is true, and another phrase of the language is added to his vocabulary. So he goes on, picking out words and meanings.

The natives have quantities of stone idols and charms, which they reverence with boundless superstition. They also have devil-kings and witch-doctors. And, as you know, they are cannibals, and several men are killed and eaten not far from the new house going up. The boy from .Aneityum, once a servant of Dr. Inglis, is much distressed that the blood has been washed into the water of a boiling spring, and no water can be found for the tea. He seems to think this is the very worst of these savage doings—they have spoiled the tea-water.

The days go on, the house is occupied, a little son brings gladness. But alas, the house is built too near the shore. Says an old chief, " Missi, you will die here. We sleep on the hills and trade-winds keep us well. You must go sleep on the hill." But before this can be done, ague and fever attack the young mother of the wee baby boy, and before long, there is a quiet grave in which mother and child lie asleep, and the broken-hearted missionary says afterwards, " But for Jesus and His fellowship, I must have gone mad beside that grave and died." He has many sweet memories. and among them the words before his wife died, "I do not regret leaving home and friends. If I had it to do over, I would do it with more pleasure, yes, with all my heart."

This picture of life in Tanna is a panorama, and we watch it as it moves. We see the good missionary's constant kindness and patience, as he lovingly tells the savages of Jesus, gathering them together as he can, bearing with them in spite of their treacheries, continual thieving, lying, and cruelties. Sometimes they pretend to be friendly, sometimes there is encouragement in the work, and then they grow fierce and abusive, and again and again try to kill the man who has come, for love's sake, to help them.

One day there comes a ship of war from England to touch at the island. "Missi, will the captain ask if we have stolen your things?" asks a frightened native. "I expect he will," answers Mr. Paton. "I must tell him the truth."

Now what a scurrying hither and yon to bring back stolen things, till men come running, this one with a pot, another with a blanket or a pan, and so they gather a great heap together. "Missi, Missi, do tell us, is it all here?" they cry. "I do not see the lid of my kettle," he says, and one answers, "It is on the other side of the island. I have sent for it; tell him not, for it will be here to-morrow."

For a while the wholesome effect of the ship's visit lasts, then is lost. The natives have a ceremony called Nahak, a sort of incantation by the sacred men, causing the death of any one made the subject of it. To carry this out, they must have some fruit, of which the victim has taken a taste. Mr. Paton, when threatened, gives them some plums, which he has tasted, and the men vainly try to work Nahak. They explain their failure by saying that Missi is also a sacred man and his God works for him.

Again and again the missionary is beset, muskets aimed at him, "killing stones" thrown, clubs raised to strike, but all in vain. He never shows fear, but stands praying inwardly, and, as by miracle, his life is spared.

But wars multiply, opposition grows, sickness wastes, and at last the faithful missionary has to escape, after unimaginable perils, and take refuge in a passing vessel. It wrings his heart to leave Tanna, but it is the only way to save his life.

And now we see the brave man travelling in Australia and elsewhere, securing money to build the mission ship *Dayspring*. Thousands listen to the story of peril and of need which he has to tell, and the money is given.

Again we look, and see him in Scotland, and it would be wonderful to follow him in his tours in which he accomplishes so much for the beloved work.

The last picture upon which we may look shows Dr. Paton returning to the New Hebrides—not alone, for he takes a devoted wife with him, and he only touches at Tanna, where he may not stay, though some who remember his teachings beg him to do so. Other missionaries finally take up the work there, and blessings follow. Dr. Paton goes to Aniwa, and here the islanders receive him

kindly. Yet they have a savage way of asking
for anything, and swinging the tomahawk to
enforce their requests.

A mission house of six rooms is finally built,
then two orphanages, a church and schoolhouses.
An old chief becomes a Christian. Many poor
creatures began to wear a bit of calico by way of
clothing—the first sign of turning in the right
way.

And sometimes very funny things happen in this
connection. Nelwang elopes with Yakin, who
has thirty other admirers, and they keep out of
the way a long time. When at last they come to
church, Nelwang is wearing shirt and kilt, but
Yakin's bridal gown is a man's drab greatcoat
buttoned tight to her heels, with a vest hung over
this. A pair of men's trousers are put round her
neck, on one shoulder is fastened a red shirt, and
on the other a striped one, and around her head is
a red shirt twisted turban-wise, a sleeve hanging
over each ear.

The thing which at last " breaks the back of
heathenism " is the sinking of a well in the island
where water is very scarce and precious. The
natives are affrighted at the thought of trying to
bring " rain from below," but Dr. Paton digs first
and then hires the men with fish-hooks, and prays
earnestly as he works, and at last water is found—
enough for all, and the natives say " Jehovah is
the true God." Triumphs of grace follow—journeys in other lands to tell the story, and in 1907
this missionary hero enters into rest.

XXXVI

CHARLOTTE MARIA TUCKER

Known as a writer by the initials "A. L. O. E." (A Lady of England)

Missionary to India at Her Own Charges (1875–1893)

THE boys and girls who lived a while before you came upon the scene, many of them now men and women, used to know the initials at the head of this chapter very well indeed. They appeared on the title-pages of interesting books for young people, and "A. L. O. E." was known and loved by thousands of readers. She was an English lady, born in 1821, but she died in Amritsar, India, in December, 1893. How did this writer of captivating stories, which made her famous, come to finish her life in that far-off land?

It was when she was fifty-four that Miss Tucker decided to become a missionary, and to go to India. It was love that constrained her, and she was so anxious to go that she went at her own expense. Before going out she studied Urdu, one of the various tongues spoken in the country. Almost as soon as she arrived upon her chosen field, she turned her thoughts towards the special work of writing stories for the natives. This certainly was an original plan, and it proved to be a very helpful one indeed. Her stories were often parables, by which she taught truth in a fascinating fashion. You know that the Orientals are, if possible, even more fond of stories, particularly parables with picturesque settings, than we are in this country. You can imagine how the stories of such a writer as A. L. O. E. would be enjoyed. The wonderful part of it was, that she found it easy to enter into the feelings and thoughts of the people, and to adapt her stories to their language and their needs.

A series of stories explaining Jesus' parables was printed in tract form so that the poorest could buy them.

Going to Batala Miss Tucker worked among the Mohammedans, the hardest class to reach. She went about among the zenanas—or apartments where the women were shut up—and on gaining admittance would sit down gracefully upon the floor, as if she were one of the women used to such a thing, and would begin by telling a story or showing a picture. Then she would go on to teach some precious lesson of truth to the curious listeners.

The boys of the high school interested this missionary very much, and she did a great deal for them. For a while she lived in the school building, once a palace.

The Sweeper class is the lowest caste in India. They are treated as if they had no souls at all. But Miss Tucker was greatly interested in these poor outcasts. She showed by her loving care that she not only believed that they had souls, but that she cared for them and wished to help them.

For eighteen years this heroic missionary gave her life, at its sunset time, to the women of India, and at seventy-two laid down the burden.

Think how long the work of the hands may live after the hands are folded. The busy pen which a loving heart kept moving, has left its traces on both sides of the sea. The fair-faced and the dark-faced boys and girls have bent above the pages which still keep alive the lovely memory of " A Lady Of England."

XXXVII

JOHN COLERIDGE PATTESON

*Famous English Oarsman, Then Bishop, and " Martyr
of Melanesia," South Sea Islands. (From About
1856 to 1871)*

A YOUNG man can be an athlete and yet become a missionary, and, very likely, be all the better missionary for it. Certainly a strong body is an excellent missionary asset.

John Coleridge Patteson was a leader in all athletic sports as a youth, and was a famous oarsman. He was a grand-nephew of the poet, Samuel T. Coleridge, and was born in London in 1827. He was finely educated, being graduated from Oxford.

The young man became a curate of the Church of England, but a year after he was ordained, sailed to the Melanesian Islands in the South Pacific. He went with the famous Bishop Selwyn, who, through a simple clerical error in making out the boundaries, was given the largest diocese ever assigned to a bishop.

On the voyage to the South Seas, Mr. Patteson studied the Maori language, and was soon able to speak it. He helped Bishop Selwyn for five years in conducting a native training school for preparing assistants. In 1861 he was made Bishop of the Melanesian Islands. After this he reduced to writing several of the island languages which had never before been written. This was a great service, for which his native ability as a linguist, and his wide studies, had prepared him.

Grammars in these languages were next prepared, and parts of the New Testament translated into the Lifu tongue.

The Bishop's headquarters were at Moto, in Northern New Hebrides, and from there he went about to other islands of his diocese in a mission ship called *The Southern Cross*. It might be said to have been fitted out by the point of a pen, for this was done by Miss Charlotte M. Yonge, the writer, with the proceeds of her book, " The Heir of Redcliffe." Was it not a beautiful thing to do ? It should be known by all who read the interesting book.

One day you might have seen the Bishop cruising among the islands, and nearing Nakapu. A boy has been stolen lately from this island by some white traders. The islanders are fiercely set upon revenge, but the good Bishop is unsuspicious. He lowers his boat from *The Southern Cross* and rows out to meet the men coming in their canoes. After their custom, they invite him to enter one of their boats, which he does, and is taken ashore. He is

never seen alive again. Search is made for the un-
returning friend, and his body is found pierced with
five wounds. So, in the year 1871, the Martyr of
Melanesia wins his crown.

His place among the hero-dead
 Who still are truly living,
This martyr takes, whose hero-life
 Gave cause for such thanksgiving.

He is but one, but he is one
 Of that great host uncounted,
Whose valorous souls, by sword and flame
 To heights celestial mounted.

Why still the moving stories tell?
 Because the tales are deathless,
And we should do far more this day
 Than listen, thrilled, and breathless.

Not to their crowns may we aspire,
But to their quenchless, high desire.

XXXVIII

SAMUEL CROWTHER

The Slave-Boy Who Became a Bishop. (*Missionary and Bishop from 1864 to 1891*)

IF you could have looked down upon the shore of Africa, in the Yoruba country, long ago, you might have seen a black boy playing about. If you had watched, you might have seen

him suddenly seized by strangers who landed from a ship, and carried off to be pushed cruelly into the hold of a Portuguese slaver. You have heard, perhaps, that long ago such wicked deeds were done, and money was made by seizing and selling as slaves the poor, helpless Africans.

Following this boy you might have seen that he was wretched enough, till, by a kind Providence, he was rescued and set free. He was taken to Sierra Leone, and one of the very first things he did was to beg a half-penny to buy an alphabet card for himself, so anxious was he to learn to read. He was such a bright boy, that in six months he learned to read, and in five years entered college, where, not long after, he was made a tutor. Could an American boy do much better?

The most important event of the boy's life was his becoming a Christian and giving himself to Christian service. Time went on, and from being a tutor, Samuel Crowther became a minister, and then, in 1864, was made a bishop. He was the first black bishop of modern times in Africa. He planted mission stations all along the banks of the Niger River. He had wonderful wisdom and tact in dealing with different people, and won their confidence in a remarkable way.

This man had also great ability. He was quite a discoverer, and was given a gold watch by the Royal Geographical Society as a reward for his travels and researches. He assisted in translating a part of the Bible and a part of the prayer-book into the language of Yoruba. Although he had learning and honour, he was one of the humblest of men. His humility increased as others appreciated him more.

One of the most intense longings of the good man's heart was to find his mother from whom he was torn as a boy, and tell her about Jesus. He could not hear anything about her, nor find her in any way.

But one day a most wonderful thing happened, although it was not too hard for God to do. A woman came to be baptized, and the Bishop examined her to see if she understood, and was ready for baptism. He found that she was indeed a Christian, but he also found that she was his own mother. It was hard to tell which of the two was more joyful, as the Bishop baptized his mother and received her into the church. He called her "Hannah, the mother of Samuel."

In 1891 this first black bishop, with his white soul, entered into rest.

His life and labours were wonderful, and his memory still blooms, like a white flower in the dark soil of Africa, the land he loved.

XXXIX

MRS. H. C. MULLENS
(*Of India*)

" The Apostle of the Zenanas " and " The Lady of the Slippers " (1845–1861)

YOU know what a zenana is, don't you? That close-shut apartment in an Indian house, where the wives of the husband are shut in, and not allowed to so much as peep out of a crack?

The women in the zenanas, whether rich or poor, have always been sadly ignorant, often very idle, with nothing to do but comb their hair, look over their jewels and talk gossip, or quarrel with each other. They have always been unhappy. How to reach and teach these imprisoned women, many of them very young, was one of the first missionary puzzles. The women could not get out, and the missionaries could not get in—that is, not for a long, long while, till the lady of this story came. If you have never heard about the "slippers" you shall hear now.

The lady was born in India. Her name was Hannah Catherine Lacroix, and she was a missionary's daughter. Her birthplace was Calcutta, and the year was 1826. Her father was intensely interested in his work, and was especially anxious about the women of India. The daughter seemed to breathe the spirit of her parents from childhood.

She had not a chance to receive a very finished education, but she was very bright, and made the best use of the opportunities that she had. She spoke Bengali very fluently, and was so intelligent, loving, and sympathetic, that when she was only twelve, she was able to help her mother by taking a class of children in the day school, started in the missionary's garden.

When about fifteen she gave her heart to the Lord Jesus, and became much more earnest about helping others to know Him. She gathered the servants and taught them, and had other classes. At nineteen she married Rev. Dr. Mullens, of the London Missionary Society, and the two were very happy together in the work they loved so dearly. The wife became so well acquainted with the language that her father said that he might be able to preach a better sermon, but his daughter could carry on conversation much better than he could. A little book that she wrote for native Christian women, was printed in twelve dialects of India.

But how about the zenana and the slippers? Well, there is a very close connection. Mrs. Mullens had great skill with her needle, and did beautiful embroidery. One day a native gentleman was visiting the house. Mrs. Mullens was working a pair of slippers. The gentleman noticed and admired her work very much.

"I should like my wife taught such things," he said, finally. Quick as a flash the missionary said,

"I will come and teach her." The slippers thus opened the way to the zenana in the first place. Next a school was planned, and by and by, after the first opportunities, the missionary ladies had access to many shut-in women, and the work grew.

In the midst of loving labours, Mrs. Mullens' life ended at thirty-five, in 1861.

The embroidery needle that she used so skillfully is lost, and the work of the busy fingers worn out long ago. Both answered their end, simple as they were. Doors are open to-day, and stand wide, against which Mrs. Mullens pushed her little needle-point.

XL

DR. CORNELIUS VAN ALAN VAN DYCK

First Translator of the Bible into Arabic, and Mission-
ary in Syria for Fifty-Five Years (1845–1895)

THE native doctors, or medicine men, in heathen lands, give the most horrible doses, and practice the most dreadful cruelties imaginable, in their efforts to drive away disease.

A missionary doctor is a great blessing in any mission field. Dr. Van Dyck was the second one ever sent to Syria by the American Board. The first one was Dr. Asa Dodge, but he died in less than two years, and for five years there was not a single American physician in the land of Syria, where once the Great Physician healed the sick and saved the sinful.

You know that the Scriptures have been called "Leaves of Healing." They are meant for all the sin-sick, but have to be given to those in heathen countries in a way that they can understand. Dr. Van Dyck was a great translator of God's Word. His name is always associated with Syria, and with

the giving of the Arabic Scriptures to the world.
Do you know that a large proportion of the heathen
world can be reached by the Arabic tongue? Missionaries tell us that this is true.

Cornelius Van Alan Van Dyck was born in the
year 1818, in Kinderhook, Columbia County, New
York. After receiving his medical education at
the Jefferson Medical College, Philadelphia, he was
appointed medical missionary to Syria when twenty-
one years of age. The first eight or ten years were
spent in teaching, visiting, preparing text-books,
and attending to the sick in all parts of the large
field. There were wars in the years 1840–1845,
and the good doctor was very busy, ministering to
the wounded and suffering, heroically forgetful of
himself.

When he was twenty-eight he was ordained a
minister of the Gospel, and was thus prepared to
preach as well as to do medical work. Later, he
was so busy going about the country, riding im-
mense distances, that it was said that "the station
was on horseback."

The translation of the Bible into Arabic was begun by Dr. Eli Smith about 1849, and he worked
diligently for eight years until his death, but was
only willing then, to be responsible for the first ten
chapters of Genesis, printed under his own eye. It
was then that Dr. Van Dyck took up the work for
which God had been making him ready in various
ways for seventeen years. He had read and mastered a whole library of Arabic books—poetry, history, grammar and the rest, and was without an

equal in command of the language. When printed the press could not work fast enough to supply the demand for Bibles.

After fifty-five busy and fruitful years in Syria, death came in 1895.

The bodies that he healed in that old Bible land have long since passed away, but the living message of the Word of God given to the people through his splendid service, still continues.

XLI

ELIAS RIGGS

Missionary to Turkey and Master of Twelve Languages
(1832-1901)

HAVE you ever stopped to think how hard it must be to learn the queer languages of foreign lands? Of course the different tongues must be learned, and learned well enough to speak and read them, or missionary work cannot be done as it should be done. The natives of other countries, especially those of degraded heathendom, cannot be taught English, so as to learn the Truth in that language. They must usually have it given to them first of all in their "mother-tongue."

Some have "the gift of tongues" in a higher degree than others, and this missionary, Elias Riggs, who went to Turkey long ago, had very wonderful ability.

He was born in New Providence, New Jersey, in the year 1810, and in his early life showed great talent in learning languages. While in college he mastered Hebrew, Syriac, Arabic, Chaldean, and modern Greek. He even made an Arabic grammar, and a Chaldean manual. To become on speaking terms with all these tongues would seem to be an heroic task to some of us. But the young student loved it, and that made it easy.

Dr. Riggs, as he was afterwards known, went first to join the noted missionary, Dr. Jonas King, in Greece, in the city of Athens. He sailed, with his wife, in 1832. After six years he was sent to Smyrna, Turkey, then to work among the Armenians, and finally to Constantinople.

During a visit to America, he was engaged as instructor in Hebrew and Greek in Union Theological Seminary. Returning to Constantinople, Turkey, he began a translation of the Bible in Bulgarian. He had added this language to those with which he was already familiar. Afterwards he helped in revising the Turkish translation of the Scriptures. This work, which became the standard translation, was printed in Armenian and Arabic characters, so that both common people and scholars could use it.

School books and devotional books, either translations or originals, kept the missionary additionally busy. He translated, or wrote in the first place, four hundred and seventy-eight hymns in the Bulgarian tongue, to say nothing of other labours.

Dr. Riggs was said to have a working knowledge of twenty languages and was master of twelve. Is it not wonderful to think of ? How many people he reached with the Truth ! It is said that four nations are now reading the Word of God as he put it into their own speech for them. His translations are read and sung by tens of thousands, " from the Adriatic to the Persian Gulf, and from

the snows of the Caucasus to the burning sands of
Arabia." The devoted missionary died in Constantinople, in 1901.

A son, Dr. Edward Riggs, born in 1844, entered
the work in Turkey, in 1869, his command of the
language being worth a great deal. His life was a
varied one, in opportunities and responsibilities, in
"journeyings oft" and perils many, robbed and
threatened, but escaping with his life, and going
on fearlessly with his work. His greatest service
was in the theological seminary, but he was so
variously engaged as to be called "The Bishop of
the Black Sea Coast." He died February 25, 1913,
after forty-four years of service, leaving five of his
seven children in the field.

XLII

ISABELLA THOBURN

Founder of the First Woman's College in India
(1869–1901)

IMAGINE ten children in one family—five boys and five girls—would there not be lively and bustling times in that home? No doubt this was true of the Thoburn home, in St. Clairsville, Ohio, where devoted and godly parents reared this flock. The mother, especially, was a wonderfully strong character who had great influence over her children.

The ninth child and youngest daughter but one, was Isabella, who was born in 1840.

There was nothing very extraordinary about her in her childhood, but she grew up to do an extraordinary work, and was well prepared for it by a very good education, and an experience in teaching, first, at the age of eighteen in a country school, and later as a teacher in two different seminaries for girls. One characteristic should be noted especially. Isabella was most faithful and thorough in everything she did. She would not leave a thing till she understood it absolutely when a student, nor till she had done her very best as a missionary.

This young woman did not grow up with the thought of going to the foreign field, but when a great need caused the call to come, she was ready, and soon made her decision.

Dr. James Thoburn, first missionary bishop in India, who has served there fifty years, was the brother who summoned his sister to the work abroad. He has had a wonderful and heroic history himself, and at one time had the greatest baptismal service in India. But there was a time, after the death of his wife, that was so filled with difficulty and anxiety, because he was so unable to do anything for India's women, and was so weighed down with their needs that he wrote to his sister, asking her to join him in the field. This she did, in 1869, to minister to those poor degraded women, "Unwelcomed at birth, unhonoured in life, unwept in death." Oh, the pity of it all!

But you are not to think that it was an easy and simple thing for Miss Thoburn to go when called and ready. There was no society in the Methodist Church to send her. She might have gone out under the Woman's Union Missionary Society of New York, but she longed most ardently to be sent by some organization in her own church, to which she was devotedly attached.

Just at this time of need, Dr. and Mrs. William Butler, founders of the Methodist Episcopal Missions in India, and afterwards in Mexico (heroic workers they), came home, with the wife of Dr.

E. W. Parker, of India. These three talked to their Boston friends about the things that burned in their hearts, and at last a meeting for organization of women was suggested and appointed. With the day came a pelting rain, and but six women gathered to meet Mrs. Butler and Mrs. Parker, who spoke as eloquently as if to hundreds. Nothing daunted, the organization of the Woman's Foreign Missionary Society of the Methodist Episcopal Church was formed by these eight brave women.

At the first public meeting it was made known that a missionary candidate was ready to be received. But there was little money in the treasury. Then a Boston lady sprang up and said, " Shall we lose Miss Thoburn because we have not money to send her ? No ! Rather let us walk the streets of Boston in calico dresses and save the money. I move the appointment of Miss Thoburn to India." The ladies cried out, " We will send her," and they did. So she went, and Dr. Clara Swain, shortly afterwards found and sent as a medical missionary, went with her.

From the beginning Miss Thoburn felt that the India girls and women must be educated, and as soon as possible began the school which grew into the famous Girls' Boarding-School and High School, and finally in 1870 into Lucknow Women's College. But the beginnings were feeble. Seven frightened girls were coaxed in, and a sturdy boy set at the door of the room with a club to keep off any intruders who might venture to interrupt the proceedings.

To this school and to this remarkable teacher came, in due time, the high caste, gifted girl, Lilavati Singh, whose father's views of education were in advance of the times. Upon one of the enforced visits home in thirty-two years of service, Miss Thoburn brought this cultivated, charming woman with her. It was in 1898. She brought this "fragrant flower of womanhood from India's garden," as sweet as ever bloomed, in order to have her plead for money for the college buildings, $20,000 being the quick response.

It was of Lilavati Singh that President Harrison said, after hearing her at the Ecumenical Missionary Conference at New York, that if *this one only* had been the result of all money spent for missions, it was well worth the whole amount.

Miss Thoburn was obliged to remain at home for some years, but they were not idle. She was for some time busily engaged with Mrs. Lucy Rider Meyer in Chicago. Mr. and Mrs. Meyer had begun their spreading work of deaconess homes and training schools. Miss Thoburn helped to "mother" the girls in training, and assisted in organizing the work later in Ohio, planning to introduce it into India. For this reason she became a deaconess herself.

The girls all loved Miss Thoburn dearly, and her work for and among them was a beautiful one. A little touch may show you that this strong and heroic character was "one of us" after all, in a way. She had an odd terror of street cars in that day, and when crossing a track would run as fast as she could, in spite of her somewhat generous avoirdupois. She said that it always seemed to her when she saw one coming, especially at night, as if it threatened, " I'll have you yet, Isabella."

Returning to India in 1900 for further devoted service, she was attacked with cholera, and went triumphantly Home in August, 1901, leaving a sorrowing multitude.

By and by Miss Singh was given large responsibilities as professor in Miss Thoburn's college, which she discharged with rare ability and devotion. She came to America to beg help in enlarging the college buildings, but died in 1909 after a serious operation. Her loving friend, Mrs. D. C. Cook of Elgin, gave her body burial and memorial, and she sleeps afar from home, but unforgotten.

XLIII

DR. ELEANOR CHESNUT
Missionary Martyr of Lien Chou, China (1893–1905)

A LETTER in a well-remembered hand lies upon the desk to-day, in which Eleanor Chesnut signed herself, in a bright little sportive way she had,

" Much love
From
Your Chiny Sister,
E. C."

You cannot know, as you read, how hard it is to write of this dear, personal friend, once a visitor in the home, and bound to the heart by the tenderest ties. But it is such a lasting joy to have known her that the story must have a jubilant note in it, all through, as it tells of her wonderfully heroic life and martyr crown. You need not be afraid to read it, for it should make you glad that such a brave soul ever lived her life of sacrifice and service.

It had a very pitiful beginning—this life we are

179

thinking about now. It began in the town of Waterloo, Iowa, on January 8, 1868. Just after Eleanor's birth her father disappeared mysteriously and was never again heard of. The mother, who had the respect and sympathy of her neighbours, died not long after, and the family, consisting of several brothers and sisters, was scattered.

Eleanor, who was but three at the time, was adopted, though not legally, by some friendly people near, who had no children. They had little money, but did the best they could for her, finding her a puzzle and a comfort both. In later years the father spoke of her " loving, kindly ways, her obedience in the family circle, and her unselfishness."

But the poor child was not happy. She was lonesome, and longed for mother-love. Well as she controlled her feelings, she did not like to be restrained, and often carried a stormy little heart within. She was happiest when in school, but when only twelve, she was distressed to find that she might have to give up study altogether. It was then that she went to live with an aunt in Missouri, in a " backwoods " country, where school privileges were of the poorest. And besides, the struggle for life was too hard to allow a chance to study, or spare anything for the expense of schooling.

The news of Park College, Parkville, Missouri, where students had a chance to earn their way, at least in part, came in some roundabout manner, and from that moment the girl made up her mind that she would go, come what might. And go she did, through the kind encouragement of the president of the college. She entered, feeling forlorn and friendless, but soon found warm friends and congenial surroundings. Her studies were a continual delight. But how to live was a problem. Her family could do little for her, and she had to take the bounty of missionary boxes, when it came to clothing. It was such a struggle to accept these supplies that she could not feel very grateful in her sensitive heart, but it was really heroic to wear the things. Don't you think so ?

These hard trials in youth had " peaceable fruits " afterwards, for they ripened into a wonderful gentleness, sympathy, tact, and understanding, which made her a blessing to others. Writing to a friend, in later years, about the poor boys in China needing clothes, she said : " The poor boys ! They are so shabby that I wish I could do more for them. I remember how shabby I was at Park College years ago. I do not mind nearly so much now, wearing old things."

Outwardly the student was brave and quiet, but there was a tumult within that was only hushed when she became a Christian. Afterwards came the determination to become a missionary. She said a pathetic thing about this decision. (How it comes back in her very tones this moment !) She said, " One thing that made me feel that I *ought* to go was the fact that there was really no one to mind very much if I did " But this was not said in a dismal, self-pitying way. The larger reason she gave at another time and place, when asked for it in connection with her appointment. She said simply that it was "a desire to do good in what seemed the most fitting sphere."

In 1888, on leaving Park College, the young girl entered upon the study of medicine. She had no great natural love for the profession, but, as she confided, it seemed as if it would add so much to her usefulness. She said that it was very hard the first year, and she wondered if she *could* go on and finish the course, but she resolved that she *would*. And she did, with a resolute will, even becoming interested in it, as she plunged heart and mind into the study that she was sure would make her more helpful. But a missionary friend, who knew her well in Lien Chou, said afterwards that this girl should have been an artist, not a doctor, if her real nature had been consulted, and that it was perfectly heroic in her to practice medicine and surgery as she did.

The medical course was taken in Chicago, with the advantage of a scholarship, but the student "lived in an attic, cooked her own meals, and almost starved," as a Chicago friend afterwards insisted. Her meals were principally oatmeal. A course in the Illinois Training School for Nurses in Chicago followed, and some money was earned by nursing in times allotted for vacations. She served as nurse to Dr. Oliver Wendell Holmes in his final illness. The training was made more complete by a winter in an institution in Massachusetts, and then came a course of Bible training in Moody Institute, Chicago.

In 1893 Dr. Chesnut was appointed as medical missionary to the foreign field, and was assigned to China. She had a strange, natural aversion to the water, but was a brave sailor notwithstanding.

After a little time at Sam Kong, studying the language, and doing some incidental work, the doctor was appointed to Lien Chou. From a letter in print this extract is taken. (You can see that she was "a saint with a sense of humour," bless her! There was some good Irish blood in her, which no doubt gave the twinkle in her brown eyes.)

"Here I am at last. I had a few things carried overland. The boats are on their way. They have divided their cargoes with several others, and are floating the hospital bed-boards and my springs. Won't they be rusty? I only hope they won't try to float the books and the organ. I don't mind being alone here at all. . . . I have to perform all my operations in my bathroom, which was as small as the law allowed before. Now, with an operating table, it is decidedly full. But I do not mind these inconveniences at all. . . . A druggist gave me a prescription which you may find useful, though the ingredients may be more difficult to procure in America than in China. You catch some little rats before they get their eyes open, pound to a jelly, and add lime and peanut oil. Warranted to cure any kind of an ulcer."

A missionary from Lien Chou lately told how Dr. Chesnut began the building of a hospital. When her monthly salary-payment came she saved out $1.50 for her living, and with the rest bought bricks. At last the Board in New York found this out, and insisted upon paying back what she had spent on bricks for the hospital. She refused to take the whole sum, saying that to do it " would spoil all her fun."

The story of the amputation of a Chinese coolie's leg without any surgical assistance has gone far and wide. The operation was successful, but the flaps of skin did not unite as the doctor hoped, and she knew that any failure in getting well would be resented by the people, and perhaps result in a mob. By and by the man recovered perfectly, and, later, the doctor secured some crutches for him from America. But, at the time, it was noticed that Dr. Chesnut was limping. There was no use in asking her why, for the slightest hint brought out the words, " Oh, it's nothing." But one of the women betrayed the truth. The doctor had taken skin from her own leg to transplant upon what the woman called " that good-for-nothing coolie," and had done it without an anæsthetic, save probably a local application, transferring it at once to the patient. What do you think of heroism like that? And then to say nothing about it!

When the Boxer troubles sent foreigners to the coast for safety, Dr. Chesnut refused to go for some months, and went at last under pressure from others, not from fear. She returned in the spring. That same season she came home on furlough, when " none knew her but to love her." A tour among societies supporting a ward in Lien Chou Hospital endeared her to many. She was so bright, so engaging, so interesting, and withal showing a sweet humility most touching. At this time she had the first silk dress ever owned. It must have been given to her!

Returning to her work for two busy, blessed years, there came the October day in 1905 when a mob, excited and bent on trouble, attacked the hospital. Dr. Chesnut, coming upon the scene, hurried to report to the authorities, and might have escaped, but returned to see if she could help others, and met her cruel death at the hands of those she would have saved. Her last act was to tear strips from her dress to bandage a wound she discovered in the forehead of a boy in the crowd. The crown of martyrdom was then placed upon her own head. "She being dead, yet speaketh."

NOTE.—The sketch of Dr. Chesnut by Dr. Robert Speer, in the book, "The Servants of the King," has furnished many of the items in this story.

XLIV

CALVIN WILSON MATEER

Founder of Shantung College, China (1863–1908)

DO missionaries need to know anything besides books, preaching, and teaching? Indeed they do, and the more things they know and can do, the better.

This famous missionary of forty-five years in China, will not only be remembered as the founder of a school that became under his care a great college and then a university, but as a man who could turn his hand to almost anything, and turn it to good purpose, too. He was master of many kinds of machinery and knew how to harness electricity to his work, in addition to skill in many other directions.

The boy who grew up to do so many things well, was born in the beautiful Cumberland Valley, not far from Harrisburg, Pennsylvania, in 1836. His father and mother were staunch, devoted, Scotch-Irish folk, who brought up their seven children "in the fear of the Lord faithfully." Although the farmer-father used to start the work of the day by having breakfast before daylight, even in summer, very often, there was always time for morning and evening family worship, and usually with singing, led by the father's fine tenor voice.

The boys and girls of this household thought it no hardship to learn the Westminster Shorter Catechism thoroughly. We know that they thought well of it, for we hear that when busy with picking out stones and bits of slate turned up by the plow, in ground none too fertile, they used to divert themselves by saying the catechism now and then, as something far more interesting—as indeed it was.

There was a mill in connection with the father's place, where he hulled clover-seed. Running water turned the wheel. As a very little boy, Calvin used to wish that he were tall enough to reach the lever and turn on more water, so as to make the wheel go faster. All his life long he was eager to turn on power, and make things "go" and "go faster" if he could, by any hard work of his own.

When the boy was five, his parents moved to a farm twelve miles north of Gettysburg, near what is now York Springs, Adams County, Pa. Here they lived till Calvin was about ready to be graduated from college. The family moved twice afterwards, finally settling in Monmouth, Illinois, but it was the Adams County home that the missionary meant when he wrote: "There are all the fond recollections and associations of my childhood." One who knows anything about Gettysburg and vicinity will agree to its being an earthly paradise, and will be glad that a missionary had a chance to grow up there.

The home was named " The Hermitage," because it seemed " far from everywhere." It was believed to be haunted by the ghost of a tenant who was buried in an old deserted churchyard a mile distant. It was said that the sunken mound would not stay filled, and also that a headless man had been seen wandering round in the dark wood at night. The Mateer children used to go to the old empty church and burying-ground in the daytime, but Calvin used to run by at night with a fast-beating heart, if obliged to pass at all. He decided that he would not give up to such fear. One night he went and sat on the graveyard fence, determined to stay till he did not feel afraid any more. There he sat while owls hooted and winds shrieked, till he felt that the victory was won. He did not know then that he was disciplining himself for things more heroic in China.

After attending school and academy, and working at home at intervals, the youth taught school when not eighteen, and looking younger, in order to help on the college education fund. Many of the scholars were older than he, and some of the boys were very rough, but the teacher held his own, and got a great deal of good discipline besides.

The thought of missionary work was in the young man's mind from boyhood, although, he said, " as a dim vision and half-formed resolution."

Yet it did not fade, but brightened with the years. It was his mother's influence very largely that strengthened it. Through the struggles for education, she kept it before all her children that they should prepare themselves to carry the Good News to the heathen, or do God's work at home.

Foreign missionary books and magazines were read in the family. Long before pretty mite-boxes were given freely by Mission Boards, Mrs. Mateer made one with her own hands (it was early in the forties) and covered the little wooden thing with flowered wall paper. It stood on the parlour mantel, an object of intense interest to the children because it meant so much to " mother." It was a delight to earn pennies, or go without things for sake of the box, and when a silver coin could be dropped in, it was a joyous occasion. Once a year the box was opened. It was a red-letter day. The mother lived to see four of her children in China.

Between college and theological seminary, Mr. Calvin Mateer took charge of an academy in Beaver. He was very successful, but the thing that we like to note in this is, that there Rev. J. R. Miller, D. D., whom so many of us knew and loved for his books and Sunday-school writings, was a pupil, and said that he owed more, perhaps, to Mr. Mateer than to any one, for the shaping of his life.

At last, after long preparation, and some trying detentions, the missionary and his bride took their way to China. They went in a sailing vessel, while the battle of Gettysburg was going on, and not till October, when overtaken by another vessel, did they know how it ended. The captain was coarse, even cruel, the accommodations were incredibly uncomfortable, but at last the voyage ended.

Then began the forty-five years of strenuous and devoted service, with but three vacations at home. Dr. Mateer had a marvellous mastery of Chinese, a great gift in adapting himself to conditions, and of making what he could not get, in the way of equipment. His wife was indeed a helpmeet. After her death and the lonely years following, the home was reëstablished, with Mrs. Ada Mateer to make it bright. (In time of the Boxer troubles she was one of those who did valiant service in making sand bags, by way of barricading the enemy.) The great Shantung College, always associated with Dr. Mateer, began as a school with six boys. Before the founder passed away there were five hundred students, and it had passed from being a college into a university, to be a lasting memorial. The missionary's literary labours were also prodigious. It is almost incredible—the number and extent of these. He died in 1908, and sleeps in China, where the great changes that he foresaw, prophesied, and, in his measure, helped to bring about, are now going on.

The veteran Dr. Hunter Corbett, of Chefoo, close friend and co-labourer, outlived Dr. Mateer, and has just now completed fifty years of service.

XLV

DR. EGERTON R. YOUNG
Missionary Pioneer and Pathfinder of Canada
(1868–1909)

I F you have never read "By Canoe and Dog train," you have a thrilling pleasure before you, which I am sure you will not put off any longer than need be. You will probably not stop  till you have read also, "On the Indian Trail," "My Dogs in the Northland," and one or two others available. They are full of wonderful adventures, told in a fascinating fashion, by the man who braved untold dangers and difficulties, to win uncounted Indians for his Master. Dear me! If only you could have heard him lecture, you would have been glad of it for a lifetime.

Mrs. Young was as heroic as her husband, when they gave up the comforts of home and parish in a civilized land, to go to the far Northland on the mission of mercy. It was in 1868 that the first journey was taken, followed by many others, quite beyond telling in this small space. They camped on prairies, forded bridgeless rivers, waded wide streams, went in canoes, sometimes carrying an ox that in his bigness sprawled over the sides, and had more hair-breadth escapes and adventures than you could count.

Mrs. Young did not always go with her husband, but often it was as heroic to stay where she did, and allow him to go over unknown trails through snow and ice and bitter cold. On their first northward journey it took two and a half months to reach their destination, Norway House. Dr. Young's parish stretched north and south five hundred miles, and was sometimes three hundred miles wide.

On his trips he slept in holes dug in the snow when it was thirty to sixty below zero. His Indian runners, sometimes twenty or more, ran beside the dog-train. Sometimes the missionary's face and feet were both bruised and bleeding. Sometimes he was wet with cold sweat which froze, and made his clothes like stiff leather. Sometimes his guides had to build a fire in the snow where their dauntless leader took off his clothes to dry them and warm his body. Typhoid fever and other illnesses sometimes followed, but as soon as he was well he took up his work once more, and was away on his travels.

Often the sunlight on the snow was so dazzling that it was impossible to travel in daytime, for fear of being blinded, and the journeys had to be made by night, under the stars. Over vast tracks he went, meeting the Indians at their council fires, and in their wigwams, talking with them and showing them the Way of life. He understood their natures well, and had great power over them.

Wild savages became gentle, horrid idols were put away, the rattles and drums of the medicine men were hushed, with their dreadful yells. Crops were raised, and the first wheat was winnowed by shaking it in sheets which Mrs. Young sewed together to hold it while the wind scattered the chaff. The missionaries lived, as did the Indians, principally on fish, 10,000 being caught and frozen in the fall, to keep the family and the dogs till April.

As the missionary's fame grew, many came begging for teaching. A chieftainess came after two weeks' journey, to spend two weeks with them, and learn the truth. She was given a calendar to show when Sabbath day came, and sent home, after faithful teaching. She begged for a visit, and received it, though it took two weeks' travel over ledges of ice overhanging a rapid river.

For some time before his death, Dr. Young gave himself up to lecturing, and enlightening others, in America, Great Britain and Australia, concerning the Indian work.

He was entertained by President Cleveland in the White House, and honoured everywhere.

His brave life ended here in 1909.

XLVI

DR. HENRY HARRIS JESSUP

Missionary in Syria for Fifty-four Years (1855-1910)

IS it not sad to think that in Syria, from which land our Bible came, the light went out long ago, and needed to be rekindled? Missionaries were needed there for this work, and you will

like to hear of one great, splendid man who spent fifty-four years of service in this old Bible Land.

In Montrose, Pennsylvania, in the year 1832, the boy was born who was to give such a long life of labour to Syria. He was the sixth of eleven children. All but one of these lived to grow up. It must have been a lively family group. It really was, and a happy one, too, with a devoted father and mother to bring them up "in the nurture and admonition of the Lord."

The father was chairman of the Platform Committee in Chicago, in the convention that nominated Abraham Lincoln for the Presidency. After the committee had done its work, Mr. Jessup and another delegate went to their room at the hotel, knelt down together, and commended it all "to God who was the Judge of all and who could give success." This shows something of the character of the father of the missionary.

It is always interesting to know how the thought of going as a missionary first came to any messenger. With Dr. Jessup it came when he was twenty, and was leading a missionary meeting. He told what he could on the subject of the hour, and urged all to support the work, adding an appeal to those to go themselves, who were able to do it. The thought suddenly came to him that it was very inconsistent in him to do that, when he was not ready to go himself. He felt that he ought to take his own advice. The Day of Prayer for Colleges strengthened the feeling, and the decision was made fully, not long after. He studied medicine as well as theology, and also dentistry, so that he might be better prepared for work. In June, 1854, he decided for Syria.

Before he went out the missionary talked to a large number of children in a meeting in Newark, N. J. He said to them: "When you go home I want you to go by yourselves, and write down this resolution: 'Resolved that, if God will give me grace, I will be a missionary.'" Thirteen years afterwards, when home on furlough, Dr. Jessup went to Newark to give the charge to a young missionary, Mr. James Dennis. He was entertained in the home of the young man's mother, who told this story: "After my boy came home from your meeting years ago, he said to me, 'Mother, I have written down that, if the Lord will give me grace, I will be a missionary.' I said, ' Jimmy, you are too young to know what you will be.' He answered, 'I did not say "I will be," but "if God will give me grace I will be a missionary." ' And now," said the mother, " you are here to set him apart to be a missionary."

Long afterwards Dr. Jessup said, "Dr. James Dennis has done more for the cause of missions than any other living man that I know. For twenty-three years we have been intimate fellow-workers in Syria." Dr. Dennis' books in Arabic and English are of untold value, especially his "Christian Missions and Social Progress." Dr. Jessup said, " God must have put it into my heart to ask the children that day to make that resolution."

In December, 1855, the sailing vessel, the *Sultana*, sailed away for Smyrna, having eight missionaries and a cargo of New England rum on board. Mr. Jessup was one of the eight missionaries, who must all have deeply regretted the cargo of rum. Mr. Jessup had to leave behind the lady who was his promised wife, on account of her ill health. It meant heroism for both, until they could be united.

In February, 1856, after a very stormy and wretched voyage, Beirut was reached, and the long term of missionary labour began. In forty-nine years seven trips home were made. On the field there was teaching, preaching, writing, journeying, organizing, and, as one of the greatest achievements, the superintending of the printing in Arabic of uncounted pages of Scripture and other helps in the tongue read by so large a portion of the unchristianized world. At home the time was largely spent in speaking to people about the field—not about the missionary, but about his field and the progress there. When, on being introduced to an audience, he was lauded for his great work, he bore it as well as he could, said nothing about it, but as soon as possible turned attention to Syria, and the people there, in all their need. He wrote modestly of himself, "I take no credit for anything God has helped me to do, or has done through me."

The great-hearted, gifted, devoted missionary that helped so many of us at home as well as abroad, fell asleep in Beirut, Syria, April 28, 1910.

Dr. Samuel Jessup

If you will notice carefully you will find that often more than one from a family goes to the mission field. Dr. Henry H. Jessup's brother Samuel, twenty months younger, inspired by his example, studied for the ministry, became a chaplain in the Civil War, and then went out to Syria in 1863.

President Lincoln offered him a consulship in that country, but he resisted the temptation, and gave up everything for sake of the work. He went about, a soldierly figure, on horseback a great deal, doing his tireless, noble work. When he was about to be removed to another station, where he would not have so much hard riding to do, the people protested. When told the reason they said,

"Then let him stay here and just *sit*, and let us come and *look* at him. That will be enough." A man of Sidon said, "When Dr. Jessup walked through the streets there was not a shopkeeper whom he passed but said, 'Our city is blessed in having such a man walk its streets.'" Little children ran after him, and were never disappointed in receiving the sweets he always carried in his pockets, to give with kindly words.

After almost fifty years of happy service, Dr. Jessup entered into rest.

XLVII

MRS. A. R. M'FARLAND
The First Missionary in Alaska (1877–1897)

HOW we love to hear of pioneers. **When** the pioneer is a woman of dauntless courage and indomitable spirit, her story is perfectly fascinating. You are certain to think

Mrs. M'Farland's history very wonderful indeed.

When the baby who was to become the first missionary in Alaska, was born in Virginia, now eighty years ago, no doubt she looked much as other babies do, and no one could guess what she would grow into. No matter for that. There was One who took care that she should be prepared for it, when her work was ready for her.

To good home training was added the very best of school advantages to be had, for the girl was sent to Steubenville Seminary, Ohio, well known in all that region for its excellence. Dr. Charles C. Beatty was the principal, and his charming wife, who was known as "Mother Beatty," mothered the girls in a delightful way. You can imagine how the writer of this story felt a few years ago, on meeting Mrs. M'Farland, to have her say: "Your mother, as a young lady, was a favourite teacher of mine in Steubenville. I have never forgotten her."

As quite a young bride, the girl's missionary work began in Illinois, where her minister-husband was sent by the Presbyterian Board of Home Missions. Afterwards, the two were sent to Santa Fé, New Mexico, the first missionaries of this Board to go there, and in that difficult field they remained seven years, till Mr. M'Farland's health broke down. A change was made to Idaho, where work was carried on among the Nez Perces Indians until May, 1876, when the husband died, and after six months of loneliness, which proved too hard to endure, the wife went to Portland, Oregon.

It was there that she heard of Dr. Sheldon Jackson's explorations in Alaska. She was eager for new work, and hard work, and when Dr. Jackson came back, just as eager to get some one to return with him to that desolate and destitute field, Mrs. M'Farland was ready to go, though no one had gone before her from America, to begin the work of teaching. When she got to Alaska she found so much to do that she had no time to think of her loneliness, or of much else besides the work that filled every hour of the day, and sometimes part of the night. She said afterwards that she never for a moment regretted going. It was a great grief to her that, after twenty years, her health failed and she had to leave the people she loved so well.

It was in August, 1877, that Dr. Sheldon Jackson and the "First Missionary" reached Fort Wrangell. There was a woman a hundred miles up the Stickeen River, who was out gathering berries for her winter supply, when she heard of the arrival. At once she was moved to put her children, her bedding and belongings of every sort in a canoe, and then she paddled home as fast as she could, to offer such help as she could give, to the new missionary. She afterwards became her interpreter.

It was rather surprising to hear a bell ringing in Wrangell, and to see an Indian going up and down the street with it. This proved to be the call to afternoon school. For there *was* a small beginning, in the way of teaching. It had been made by Philip MacKay, a Christian native from Canada, who had begun it the year before, in answer to the piteous cry for help which had reached him when he came to the place to cut wood. He belonged to the Methodist Mission at Fort Simpson. Seeing the degradation in Fort Wrangell, he stayed to teach as best he could, and had a little school which he handed over to Mrs. M'Farland, and came to it himself. His original name was Clah, and he was about thirty years old.

There were thirty scholars on that August day upon which the newcomer began her school, the Indian woman, who came back a hundred miles to help her, doing her best as an interpreter. In the afternoon Clah preached in the Tsimpsean dialect, the sermon being interpreted into the Stickeen language.

The first schoolroom was an old dance hall, and the new teacher began with four Bibles, four hymnbooks, three primers, thirteen first readers, and one wall chart. Nothing daunted, she went on, with such native help as she could get, and taught the ordinary elementary English branches.

This, the only Christian white woman in the country, soon became "nurse, doctor, undertaker, preacher, teacher, practically mayor, and director of affairs generally," for all came to her for every sort of thing. People outside began to hear of her, and to beg for help from her. One old Indian from a far-away tribe came to her and said: "Me much sick at heart, my people all dark heart, nobody tell them that Jesus died. By and by my people all die and go down—dark, dark."

You can think how such appeals broke the missionary's heart, when she could do nothing to answer them. She kept writing home, begging for a minister, a magistrate, or a helper for herself, but in vain. The mails came by steamer once a month, and we have a pathetic picture of the lonely woman going down to the shore to watch the incoming boat, hoping that there might be a helper aboard, or a letter promising one. But month after month she watched in vain.

And she was alone, for as soon as Dr. Jackson could finish his own special business he sailed away, and left Mrs. M'Farland in the midst of a thousand Indians, with few white men, and no soldiers, for the military force had been withdrawn.

Mrs. Julia M'Nair Wright, the author, says about

this: "Perhaps the Church at home never had a greater surprise than when it heard that work in Alaska was begun, and a Christian, cultivated woman left there to carry it on.

"'What!' was the cry that met Dr. Jackson, 'did you leave Mrs. M'Farland up there alone among all those heathen, up there in the cold, on the edge of winter?' 'Yes,' was the reply, 'I did. And she has neither books, nor school-house, nor helpers, nor money, nor friends—only a few converted but untaught Indians, and a great many heathen about her. Now what will you do for her?'" The situation was really awakening.

Dr. Jackson's words and Mrs. M'Farland's interesting letters finally bore fruit, and money was raised for a home for the girls who were orphans, or who were rescued from worse than orphanhood.

Among the girls first received into the home were Tillie Kinnon, then fifteen, and Fannie Willard, both of whom became missionaries to their own people in due time, and have been well known in this country as well as their own.

One day two girls from the school were captured and accused of witchcraft, which meant torture, and perhaps death. The natives were having a "devil dance" when Mrs. M'Farland set out to face them and rescue the girls. Her scholars implored her not to go. "They will kill you," they cried. Her interpreter embraced her with agonizing tears and tried to hold her back, but, while even the converted Indians feared to go near, the intrepid woman went alone, faced the half-insane dancers with no show of fear, demanded the release of the girls, threatening the men with United States' vengeance, and using every imaginable argument and plea.

After some hours thus spent, she had her way. One of the rescued girls was afterwards caught and put to death, but the other was saved. At another time she had a terrible experience in facing a charge of witchcraft made upon one of her girls, but she stood her ground and saved the girl. When the money for a permanent building for the M'Farland Home was actually forthcoming, the missionary wrote, "There has been a song in my heart ever since the mail arrived, telling of the response to the call for funds. I felt sure that if we trusted Him God would, in good time, send the help we so much needed."

In 1878 Dr. S. Hall Young came to the field, where he has been so usefully engaged ever since, with the fearlessness and boundless enthusiasm that has outlasted his young manhood. He relieved Mrs. M'Farland whenever he could, taking the teaching work, while she, called "The Mother," trained the scholars in cooking, washing, ironing, mending, and all housewifely arts. Mrs. Young also taught, after her arrival, till the coming of Miss Dunbar to be a permanent assistant. So the helpers came, one by one.

After twenty years' service, Mrs. M'Farland came home, broken in health, yet able to tell to many the inspiring story of Alaska Missions, till she "fell on sleep" October 19, 1912.

XLVIII

SHELDON JACKSON

*Pathfinder and Prospector in the Rocky Mountains and
Apostle to Alaska (1858-1909)*

A MAN must needs be a hero to be worthy of such a long title as that. Do you not agree? But you will think that he earned it, if you will try to count up half the things that

he did, and endured, in over fifty years of home missionary work, and in nearly a million miles of travel, filled with the wildest adventures and escapes imaginable. Indeed, you could not imagine them if you tried, and therefore you must hear about them.

The baby who was to become such a wonderful travelling missionary, saw the light in the little village of Minaville, in the Mohawk Valley, New York State, May 18, 1834. His mother's maiden name being joined to his father's, he became Sheldon Jackson. He had two narrow escapes as an infant, once being saved from rolling into the big fireplace with logs ablaze, and once being carried from the house which was ablaze.

While Sheldon was still a baby, the father, Mr. Jackson, removed, with his wife and child, to Esperance, ten miles from Minaville, between Albany and Buffalo. Here, when the little boy was about four, the parents united with the Presbyterian Church, and afterwards dedicated the child to God in baptism, and, in their own hearts, consecrated him to the ministry. The boy himself grew up with no other thought in his mind, and while he was a "genuine boy" and had fun as other boys did, the expectation of being a minister, kept him from some boyish follies that he would have been sorry for afterwards. He said so himself, and thankfully, too. Very early the thought of being a minister was joined, in the boy's mind, with the hope of becoming a missionary.

When he was six, his father's health caused him to give up his business and move to a farm in Florida County, where the son grew up in a "house of plenty," and a happy home, giving most of his time to study, but helping with the chores. For eighteen years the family kept up membership in the Esperance church, and week by week, drove to service over a rough and hilly road, often blocked with snow in winter for weeks at a time. With breakfast over at daylight in winter, the start was made, the buffalo robes, ax, shovel, lunch basket and all, packed in, with hot soapstones and thick oak planks. Lunch was eaten at noon, but the family did not get home on short days till dark. Sometimes they were upset in the drifts, but they always got out somehow, and nobody minded.

From his early childhood the boy Sheldon was familiar with stories of the Indian wars in the Mohawk and Schoharie Valleys of New York; and the fascinating histories of David Brainerd, and David Zeisberger, and their Indian work, charmed him. Besides these, he had Bunyan's "Pilgrim's Progress," Washington Irving's works, and some of Walter Scott's stories to read. He enjoyed these very much, and early began to dream dreams of the great world outside, and to see visions of what was to be done, while wondering what his part would be.

At fifteen, the boy went to an academy at Glen Falls, N. Y., and afterwards to Union College, Schenectady, where he was "a conscientious student and a delightful companion." At nineteen, the young man was received into the church, and three months later, largely through his influence, his only sister took her stand with him. At this time seemed to begin that great longing to help others and win them for his Master, which became his passion by and by.

This hero in the making, who was afterwards to brave perils by land and sea and snow, was far from being an athlete, and was never trained in what is called " the manly art of self-defense." As a lad he was slender, physically small, often suffered in health, and was troubled with weak eyes. He was naturally averse to "rough and tumble" exercise, and his fitness for the mastery in dealing with Indians, with roughs in mining camps, and the frontiers far and near, did not depend upon physical prowess. In the fortieth year of his unique missionary work, somebody described Dr. Jackson as " short, bewhiskered, and spectacled, but by *inside* measurement a giant." Anybody who tried to combat him, found him a "giant inside," but with a heart tender as a woman's. He never knew what it was to give up when he knew he was right, and wanted to win his way.

One time at a meeting the one in charge thought that a great giant of a Tennessean near, was Dr. Jackson who was about to speak, and introduced him as "My stalwart friend from the Rockies." When the little doctor appeared almost everybody laughed, and so did he, saying, "If I had been more stalwart in height I could not have slept so many nights on the four-and-a-half-foot seat of a Rocky Mountain stage." Maybe it was his capacity for doubling up, that made a stage-driver say of him once, "He was the hardiest and handiest traveller I ever was acquainted with."

Four days before his twenty-third birthday, the student was licensed to preach, and for a few months served for the American Systematic Benevolence Society. But his heart was set on foreign missions, and he offered himself to the Board, hoping to be sent to Syria or Siam, or to South America. But the examining doctor said that his health would not allow him to go. "They thought I was not strong," he said himself, "but I had an iron constitution, with the exception of dyspepsia." Some folk would have thought dyspepsia a big enough exception to excuse a man from frontier work, but not so Sheldon Jackson. Later, a friend wrote of him, " Compared with what he has done, work in Siam would have been 'flowery beds of ease.' He can endure more hardship, travel, exposure, and hard work this minute, than half the college football players, and looks ten years younger than his sixty-four years." This is getting ahead of our story, but you won't mind. It seems to come in here, with the refusal to send the young man to the foreign field.

Work among the Indians, in Indian Territory, was the first that offered after the seminary course at Princeton was finished, and the young minister was ordained. On his twenty-fourth birthday he was married, and, on the wedding journey, the bridal pair met the rest of the Jackson family at Niagara Falls, on their way to Galesburg, Illinois, a new college town that had grown up on the prairie, and was then " just twenty-one."

The work among the Choctaws, and representatives of other tribes, was very arduous, and Mrs. Jackson, besides helping in many ways, substituting for teachers, keeping the house, and so on, found her hands full and her time, too, with " keeping the little Indians in repair."

Serious illnesses, and other circumstances, convinced Mr. Jackson that he should undertake more varied work, and in due time he was commissioned to a parish 13,000 miles square, being given oversight, as a home missionary, of Minnesota, and Wisconsin almost wholly, with nineteen preaching-places in Minnesota alone, a hundred miles apart.

A salary of three hundred dollars was his recompense for all this labour, " in journeyings oft," averaging for one quarter, thirteen and one-half miles a day, horseback or afoot. His escapes from freezing, in fierce blizzards and huge snow-drifts, would make a chapter by themselves at this time. But he did not freeze—save fingers and toes, or perhaps his nose, and he thawed out, and went on with this pioneer work.

We can't follow this active man step by step, but shall have to take flying leaps. We next find him engaged in a larger field, and more general work. It began in Iowa, and, before it was fully planned, came the Hilltop Prayer-meeting, which ought to be remembered as a companion to the Haystack Prayer-meeting long before. Mr. Jackson and two minister-friends, went up to the top of a very high bluff called Prospect Hill, on the edge of Sioux City, Iowa, there to look over the land. Part of Iowa, Nebraska, South Dakota and Minnesota were visible. Beyond, stretched nine territories, for California was then the only state west of the Missouri River, and farther on was Alaska. It was a field of 1,768,659 square miles, almost half the United States, with tens of thousands of Indians, with demon-worshipping Eskimos, with pagan or half pagan races beyond count.

The hearts of the three on the hilltop were moved to cry out to God to lead those who had power, to send out missionaries to this great field. Soon after this sacred hour, Mr. Jackson was appointed Superintendent of Missions for Western Iowa, Nebraska,

Idaho, Dakota, Montana, Wyoming and Utah, and
as far beyond as the jurisdiction of the Presbytery
of Iowa might extend.

Now began the million mile journey of the Pathfinder. "He went, on horseback or afoot, over un-
speakable roads, bumping along in ox carts, by
buckboard, stage, with mule team, by broncho,
reindeer sledge, lumber wagon, ambulance, by
freight or construction train, by dugout, launch,
steamer, canoe, revenue-cutter or cattle-ship."

"Five times the stage was robbed just before he
passed over the route; once there was only the mo-
tion of a finger between him and death, as a half
dozen revolvers were pointed at him; once he escaped scalping by the Apaches by a few hours;
again he went unharmed, when his steamer was fired
into by hostile Indians; again a fanatical papal
mob threatened his life, and once he was imprisoned
for the Gospel's sake, and set free by the President."

Under the trees, under the stars, in log huts, in
miners' camps, in dugouts and sod houses, the missionary went preaching and visiting, and organizing
churches.

A good part of the time he collected the money
needed. What he called "The Raven Fund," for
supply of pressing needs, mounted into the thousands. Nothing discouraged the dauntless soul.
Where he heard the call of need he went, with
fearless faith and indomitable courage. Railways
and stage lines gave him free transportation for
long journeys, thinking it a good investment. For

a long time his family lived in Denver, and he made sixteen round trips, to and from his home, in five years.

And now the call came to far Alaska. The exploring tour, with unimaginable dangers and terrifying difficulties was made, in spite of discouraging views of the majority, who thought there was no use in it, and no hope in it. But Dr. Jackson knew better, and was neither dismayed nor delayed by what people thought. He opened mission stations; he took Mrs. M'Farland from Portland to be the first woman worker in that strange field. He even went to Point Barrow, the northernmost place, where Siberia could be seen in the distance, and founded a mission there, where there are twenty-four days of night, and the mail comes once a year.

Government made him General Superintendent of Education in Alaska.

And now listen to the story of the reindeer. In pity for the poor Eskimos, and with a wise thought for their help, Dr. Jackson, after great efforts and prodigious discouragements, finally imported reindeer from Siberia, with native herders, and, after proving that it could be done, received government aid. Now these animals, that find their own food in the moss under the snow, and can travel where dogs cannot, and can furnish food and skin-clothing also, have proved such a boon to Alaska that Dr. Jackson would be remembered had he done nothing else. His heroic life ended in 1909.

XLIX

ROLL-CALL OF LIVING HEROES

DO you think for one instant that the heroic souls, ready to do and dare everything with dauntless courage, have all passed away, having finished their work? You cannot think so, for you know better. "The workman dies, but the work goes on," because God has always a worker ready to take it up and carry it on. There are thousands of intrepid missionaries, at home and abroad, to answer to a roll-call of living heroes.

The list of the heroes of the past is very long and we need to know the names and deeds of those who toiled in the beginning, and laid foundations. That is the reason that in the study of missions we begin with those who have gone before. The Lord Christ says to those now upon the field, "Other men laboured, and ye have entered into their labours." We ought to know the whole story, and put it together in the right way. This is one good reason for making a long list of names that belong to the past. Another is that, for the present, every one of us has a chance to see for ourselves what the heroes are doing in the world. History is in the making, and we can watch the process. The more we know of the beginnings, the more will we care to watch the progress of things. Every wide-awake young person will care to do this. One who does not "care" in these days, must surely be asleep, and would better wake up at once, for fear of missing the splendid things that are going by, and going on.

In order to suggest the looking up of those whose acquaintance we ought to make in the present, suppose we call the names of a very few of the living, now in easy reach. And then—since a large library would not hold them, suppose every reader takes pains to add to the list for private use. What a superb thing it will be, in the end. The search itself will be stimulating, and very easy, too. If you give ever so *little* attention to the matter, you simply cannot help seeing and hearing something about present-day heroes and heroines, and the *more* you give, the more worth while and thrilling it will grow to be.

To make a beginning, let us take the name of

WILLIAM DUNCAN
" The Hero of Metlakahtla "

Think of the young travelling salesman in London, giving up his excellent position to go to preach Christ to the Indians of British Columbia. He spent months in reaching Alaska ; he repeated his first sermon nine times in one day ; he founded a Christian Temperance village in Alaska ; he was followed by hundreds of Indians to the settlement of Metlakahtla, and then to Annette Island, all of whom signed a covenant not to drink, swear, break the Sabbath, cheat, lie, or do any such unchristian thing.   Everybody goes to church in Mr. Duncan's colony.

Rev. Charles Cook
Missionary to the Pima Indians

This is another living hero, who, in 1870, hearing from an army officer the sad condition of the Pimas, gave up his German church in Chicago, and, without money enough for the whole journey, or any pledged support, set out to help the poor Indians. He took a Bible, a rifle, a small melodeon, and some cooking utensils with him, and for a long time was self-supporting.   Now the largest church in Sacaton is that of the Pimas, with over five hundred members, and it is one of seven or more, gathered by Mr. Cook.

Dr. Wilfred T. Grenfell
" The Hero of Labrador "

This missionary doctor has a parish of over 2,000 miles of storm-swept coast along the Northern Atlantic. He goes his rounds among his fisher-folk by boat and dog-train, according to the season ; and, no matter what the storm or peril by land or sea, he answers each call of distress, at any cost. He " goes about doing good," as his Master did, and with an abounding joy in the work that is contagious. He has been decorated by his appreciative English Government.

Bishop Rowe
Diocese of Alaska, Protestant Episcopal Church

" From Ketchikan in the South, to St. John's in the Wilderness, beyond the Arctic Circle, the good

Bishop has set a chain of twenty mission stations, including hospitals and reading rooms." His work means perilous mountain climbing, ice-baths at un-expected times and places, long runs on snow-shoes, ahead of his dog-sledge, and many a night in a hollowed-out snow-bed, under the stars and flaming Northern Lights.

HELPERS FARTHEST NORTH

We cannot even imagine what it has meant to hold the mission stations at Point Barrow, and St. Lawrence Island, with mail but once a year, or twice at most. There it took a year or two for a broken sewing-machine shuttle to be replaced, and other supplies must take time in proportion; there, in the long Arctic night, native children must be roused from sleep to come to school, by bell or knock, and must flounder through the snow to the mission house at what would be nine o'clock in the morning for us. Dr. and Mrs. Marsh, Dr. and Mrs. Spriggs, Dr. and Mrs. Campbell, ought to be more than mere names to us, as we associate them with these regions farthest north.

MISS KATE M'BETH

Missionary and Theological Instructor Among the Nez Perces

Following her heroic sister, Susan M'Beth, who trained such noble young Indians for the ministry among their own people, Miss Kate still lives and labours with indomitable courage and enthusiasm, among the red men of the Far West. The students she has trained have acquitted themselves creditably in severe examinations, and have been faithful and fruitful in service, in many fields.

Miss Mary Reed
Missionary to Lepers in India

The world that remembers Father Damien's isolation of himself for sake of service among the outcast lepers, cannot forget this gentle, but lionhearted woman, still living, loving and labouring among the same class. Few have not heard of her discovery of the disease in her own body, when home on furlough from her India field, and the heroic leave-taking without a kiss of good-bye, as she returned to devote herself to the lepers, sharing her secret with one sister only, that she might explain afterwards, the dread reason for the sudden departure from home and friends.

Dr. Mary Stone
Native Medical Missionary in Kiu Kiang, China

Imagine a frail little woman of less than a hundred pounds avoirdupois, with a parish of many thousand souls—and bodies, with no other physician to minister to their bitter needs with medical and surgical skill. Hear the secret of her marvellous endurance, unfaltering courage, and loving service : " How is it," asked a friend, " that you can possibly bear the tremendous responsibilities that rest on you all the time, and keep on with your work, day after day ? " This was her answer : " I could not keep up or keep on, but for the fact that every morning, before the duties begin, I manage somehow, to get *a look into the Face of Jesus first*, and everything grows easy then."

DR. SAMUEL A. MOFFETT
Pioneer Missionary to Pyeng Yang, Korea

The Central Church in this, the largest city of the Land of Chosen, has sent out thirty-nine other churches in a period of fifteen years. In the home church, a congregation of over fifteen hundred on the Sabbath day and from nine hundred to a thousand at the mid-week prayer-meeting, is the ordinary thing. When Dr. Moffett began his pioneer work, which now shows such marvellous growth, he was mobbed and stoned, and every effort was made to drive him from the city. As he passed along the streets of " the oldest and wickedest city in the land," as it was then called, men and boys shouted after him, " Look at this black rascal. Why did he come here ? Let us kill him." But they could not kill or exile him, and he has lived to see one of those who threw stones at him, become an earnest Christian helper. The intrepid missionary is still " in labours more abundant."

DR. MARY P. EDDY
Of Syria

This wonderful woman, the first to be recognized and allowed to practice as a physician by the Turkish government, still goes her rounds of mercy and

healing with superb courage and utter self-forget-
fulness. It would be hard to count up the lives
saved, and the souls won by her years of devoted
service. Her more recent enterprise has been the
founding of a sanatorium among the pines, for cast-
aways, and helpless if not hopeless cases. Here
she has invested all her own savings, and uses her
monthly stipend for the place, and pitiful patients.
She prays that before she dies, she may see her
hope for a permanent home fulfilled. Her sight is
failing, and she can barely see to write her letters
of appeal, but she says: " I am going to keep on
doing and working, just as dear Dr. Samuel Jessup
did, until the end comes, or my labours are no
longer needed for these destitute sufferers."

In Siam and Laos

It has been said that this field is second only in
importance and opportunity at present to Korea.
We ought to associate some names with this part
of the Orient. There is Dr. M'Kean who is toiling
persistently and heroically for the poor lepers,
hitherto neglected. And Dr. Cort is investing his
life without stint, day and night, under mountains
of difficulty. Dr. Briggs is another name that
stands for unmeasured service, and Rev. J. H. Free-
man has been exploring new sections of the field.

How many can *you* add to this suggestive roll,
Of those afar and near, who pay the hero's toll ?

L

MISSIONARY SAYINGS
That Have Become Classic

PRAYER and pains, through faith in Jesus Christ, will do anything.—*John Eliot.*

We are playing at Missions.—*Alexander Duff.*

Now let me burn out for God.—*Henry Martyn.*

The prospects are bright as the promises of God. —*Adoniram Judson.*

The end of the exploration is the beginning of the enterprise.—*David Livingstone.*

I have seen in the morning sun, the smoke of a thousand villages where no missionary has ever been.—*Robert Moffat.*

Expect great things from God ; attempt great things for God.— *William Carey.*

I'll tell the Master.—*Eliza Agnew.*

The word discouragement is not in the dictionary of the kingdom of heaven.—*Melinda Rankin.*

Let us advance on our knees.—*Joseph Hardy Neesima.*

The world is my parish.—*John Wesley.*

Keep to work ; if cut off from one thing take the next.—*Cyrus Hamlin.*

I die for the Baganda, and purchase the road to Uganda with my life.—*Bishop Hannington.*

I will go down, but remember that you must hold the ropes.— *William Carey.*

God helping me, I will go myself.—*Melinda Rankin.*

We can do it if we will.—*Samuel J. Mills.*

Oh, that I could dedicate my all to God. This is all the return I can make Him.—*David Brainerd.*

AUTHORITIES CONSULTED
In Preparing Hero-Sketches

" Great Men of the Christian Church," Professor Williston Walker, of Yale.

" Saints and Heroes," Dr. Hodge.

" Life of Dr. John Paton," edited by his son, Rev. James Paton.

" Life of Dr. Marcus Whitman," Rev. Myron Eels.

" Life of Dr. Sheldon Jackson," Rev. Robert Laird Stewart.

" Life of Dr. Calvin Wilson Mateer," Rev. D. W. Fisher, D. D.

" Servants of the King," Dr. Robert E. Speer.

" Cyclopedia of Missions," Dwight, Tupper and Bliss.

" Who's Who in Missions," Belle Brain.

Three volumes, " Missionary Annals."

" Effective Workers in Needy Fields," five writers—Drs. M'Dowell, Mackay, Oldham, Creegan and Davis.

The Missionary Review.

Also—Mission Board leaflets, press gleanings, private letters, and personal reminiscences.